The
Secret Power
of You

Thank you for being you.

Terrie Christine

The Secret Power of You

A Guide to Mastering Your Inner Greatness

Terrie Christine

I dedicate this book to my BFF, Maira Arnaudo,
and my two conscious living daughters, Samantha and Storm.

Without you Maira, I never would have felt compelled to accomplish this feat.
Your consistent love and guidance catapulted me to the end result.
I am honored and grateful to be chosen as your friend.

And my beautiful, endlessly loving daughters, Samantha and Storm.
Both of you equally brighten my life. Living in Mom's world can be interesting,
yet you both stand by me with your loving arms wide open.

CONTENTS

Foreword

This book you have chosen to read contains some of the most deliberate principals available to you on the development of your intuition. We appear to live our lives disconnected from our internal mechanism that feeds our direction. Rather than taking the time to reflect on our inner core for answers, we have chosen to complain and blame our pains and boundaries on other people, other places or other things. We have forgotten that our very own existence is a direct result of our environment and we blindingly search for the answers to "why" only to find ourselves running on a hamster wheel.

What we consider as our real world experiences hold the triggers to bring forth subconscious occurrences that influence our present responses. As Ralph Waldo Emerson said "The intuition of the moral sentiment is an insight of the perfection of the laws of the soul." We are perfect. Perfect within the deepest level of our spirit. Within this perfection we cross pollinate our trusted intuition with our hidden limiting beliefs.

Terrie Christine has profoundly moved and inspired me with her gift to connect acutely to her intuition. She strikes a chord in your psyche that assures you that many of your own gifts and talents are easily accessible if only you take the time to trust, be mindful, live fearlessly and with gratitude.

Immediately upon reading and assimilating this book, you will have the tools to connect to the secret power of you. You will appreciate with a new sense of knowing what an amazing life form you truly are and you will be impressed at how simple it is to shift your mindset. When I read this book, I thoroughly embraced many of the how-to's as affirmations within my life. I have tremendous affection and support for Terrie and have welcomed her into my own circle of loved ones as she has cleared and healed a profound block from my past.

As an Intuitive Life Coach, she has used these same techniques she teaches in this book to help you master your ability to heal from the past. I feel with utmost sincerity that the contents you read in this results-driven collection have given me a whole new appreciation of how my intuition guides my very desires and inspires me to keep living in unconditional love.

Your direct, conscious living is tied together by your subconscious stories. The ideas here are so simple, yet powerful. My friend Terrie Christine has gifted all of us a master guide for releasing our past and placing us in the direction of happiness. As you read, embark on a journey to emotional freedom offered to you by one of the most authentic and heart-centered individuals I have the privilege of knowing.

I urge you to read this book and perform the exercises for yourself. You will gain a new perspective on how you can change your own life.

Terrie, it is a pleasure and honor that you asked me to write this forward and to celebrate you in gifting this healing work to the world.

Dr. Fabrizio Mancini
International Bestselling Author of The Power of Self Healing,
Speaker and Media Expert

Introduction

We all understand the term "rock bottom" and have seen the signs of it everywhere; a homeless man, a river so polluted fish cannot live, and news reports of war and famine. Dangerous situations abound. But of course, rock bottom will never happen to you or me. Look at us! We are professional, carry much responsibility, live in a nice house and work hard. We are, from the outside looking in, the American dream.

But what's on our insides? In the places we cannot see, in the countless people we interact with all day long—including ourselves—misdirected fear, anger, frustration and rage threaten to pull us deeper into chaos and sorrow. Most feel powerless to stop the feelings, spiraling downward, and feeling sad, confused and out of control. You clamor over the slippery razor-sharp edges of your own negative emotion. As this continues, the black hole deepens; it seems to grow larger on its own, taking over. There you are, falling onto the jagged chaos below. That's it, rock bottom, the point where you realize there is nowhere to go but up.

I now realize that life gives you experiences so you can grow and expand. I still remember when I was at the end of my 14-year relationship with the father of my children. I felt lost, without hope, lonely, frustrated and depressed. The experience I went through, and that which you may be going through can be so painful you feel as if you have nothing left.

Looking back today, I know that I had to experience such pain so that it would catapult me to the life I live today.

From that intense pain, I have been able to fully connect to all the love I have for myself, release my own limiting beliefs and help others free themselves from their own internal lies, frustrations, fears and heartache.

From that moment, when I heard the Universe speak to me, I began to search for ways I could continue to feel love within me and around me. Those words spoken to me as I laid on that bathroom floor gave me a sense of knowing that I was not done on this Earth yet.

Now, after years of mastering intuition and energy work and having helped thousands of people the world over, I am going to synthesize for you how lasting transformations occur so that you too can begin taking the first steps towards creating the life you dream of.

Relationships, disappointments and financial stress can go from being uncomfortable to unbearable. The result of just "dealing with it" can cause that frustration, hurt and pain to be so intense that you feel like you spiral into an endless hole. And worse, the longer you "deal with it" the further you move from your core self into a place of confusion, not knowing who you are or what you want in your life.

Now more than ever, it's important to start taking care of you. The quote, "The best place to find a helping hand is at the end of your own arm," says it perfectly. When you need to do something for yourself, YOU are the ONLY one who knows what YOU need. And as simple as it may sound, it can be incredibly difficult to both identify what it is you need and to then do it for yourself.

Sometimes change can feel as though it is impossible. You tell yourself that you tried in the past and no matter what you have done, it just did not work. It is important though to look at the situation with more scrutiny. What were you focusing on? Are you the type of person who gets into their comfort zone and, before you know it, 5 years have passed and you are still struggling with the same situation, still disappointed in how it turned out and still complaining about it?

The majority of people who come to me seeking help do so because they are tired of feeling like they are swimming upstream. They are tired of struggling, and tired of feeling empty, lonely and dull. When they lay their heads down to sleep at night, they are tired not only from the day's chores, but from the weight of being out of alignment with the core of who they are.

My Breaking Point

I woke up knowing I had just opened my eyes before the alarm clock went off. It was the middle of the night. I looked over at him, the father of my children, laying next to me only to feel in my gut the emptiness and despair I could no longer ignore. My soul longed to feel the love from him I had not felt in the previous 7 years. This night was not unlike all the other nights of the past year where I found myself laying down to sleep at night, closing my eyes and welling up with tears. I would sob in silence, the tears flowing hard and wetting the pillow, all while I pretended to be asleep.

I sat up slowly to slip out of bed and move quietly into the bathroom. Each step I took threw me deeper into the gut-wrenching agony of emptiness. I laid down on the cold tiles of the bathroom floor and began asking the Universe to take me. I did not want to be here. I had lived with this pain long enough and I had nothing left to give.

Through my tears, I repeated in my head "I no longer want to be here. I no longer want to live. If I don't have love in my life, there's nothing here for me." The words echoed in my head as I repeated them over and over.

After some time, the sound of the words began to change and I began to feel a strange sense of calmness. My body began to feel as if it was floating. With my eyes closed, I could see stars so close I thought I could touch them. My senses became heightened and I could taste a sort of dampness in this space.

Time and space stood still and then I heard the words loud and clear: LOVE WILL COME... Those words echoed through every ounce of my being and every cell of my body. I felt the length of my body tingle. And I instantly knew my life had changed.

Intense Emotion and a Breakthrough

After so much suffering, I had finally realized my happiness was never his responsibility.

You cannot expect other people to provide your sense of self. This deceptive thinking creates a false sense of hope; you simply increase your feelings of powerlessness, anger and loss when you expect others to create the life, love and meaning you believe he or she can provide .

It's not their job. It's yours.

I have learned just how to obtain this Secret Power of You from many years of personal experience, practice, and helping others achieve this for themselves. Being able to find my power saved me from a cycle of broken expectations and dreams. It saved me from the programmed patterns of destructive thinking. It saved me from prolonged suffering.

I personally know this because it took me so very long to recognize this for myself. I do not want you to waste as much time as I did realizing that only we are capable of satisfying our own desires, wants, and needs. It is essential that this fulfillment come from within. It was right there on that bathroom floor that I began to find my own light, my own energy and power. Immediately, I could work my way into my best life. That's what I want for you.

What happened on that bathroom floor exactly? I confronted my personal history, the repetitive behaviors hoping for a different outcome, the anger, the endless arguments with no conclusion, the resentments and the feeling of a lack of love. How had I gotten to this point? It was as if I had built a cage and crawled inside to suffer in the exact same way until the end of time. Obsessive, circular thoughts occupied much of my mind. My painful relationship built walls inside me and out. I was cut off from my own feeling, from the world. I had to change.

I asked myself one question: What adjustments can I make within myself to change my outcome? The answers were complicated and painful, but as I overcame fear (the pain of my daily life was simply too much), I could look at myself objectively.

I admitted I was fighting with things beyond what I could see within myself. I was deeply depressed. As I began to dig my way out, I took every tool I could find and began turning my "why me's" into "how's". Reflection, meditation and mindfulness became important to me and will also become important for you.

I acknowledged to myself how I participated in my own unhappiness. I also realized that I had completely repressed my powerful intuition—we are all given this internal compass—and the conflict within me was exhausting. Acknowledging, honoring and developing that intuition saved me. It can save you, too.

Intuition is the tiny voice inside of you that says "Yes! This is right!" or "No! Don't do it!"—and your job is to pay attention and take guided action So many of us convince ourselves, despite the little voice, that a different approach—someone else's approach—is the right thing. From partners and spouses to friends and bosses, people around you will attempt to exert influence. That's human interaction and common behavior. However, when you live heart-centered, it's your job to listen to your inner voice, access what feels good for you and determine your course forward. You are the captain of your own ship and, to feel good within yourself, you need to stand on the bridge and set your own course; chart a path that will give you the space around yourself to really hear your own needs. That voice is intuition, a priceless gift given to all of us at birth.

As I felt my own intuitive voice rise, I began to see its absence in so many lives. I started working with clients, teaching them my methods to reach their own voice and harness their power on the inside. No looking back on "woulda, coulda, shoulda." I wanted to show them how mastering the self could change their daily struggles. I asked them to acknowledge what was happening in their lives and how they contributed to the difficulties. I then asked them to listen to their innate intuitive voice and tell me what it was saying. Many were surprised by what they heard. That's how good they were at denying their own happiness and peace of mind.

When you find the power to fulfill your own needs and desires, to listen to your own internal voice, your individual "music" that no one else knows how to play but you, it brings a sense of clarity that you have never felt before. You begin to have a clearer vision of who you are, what you want, where you want to be and exactly how to get there. You will see strength you never knew you had, a limitless capacity for love and a new-found sense of peace. Self-acceptance and inner love is the key to the Secret Power of You.

Since that time, I have studied with masters of meditation, energy work, intuitive development and several other modalities. With due diligence and process, the answer to my struggles came to me in the words, "love will come." Today, I use my education and personal experience to identify the barriers within others that prevent them from accessing prosperity, clarity, comfort, love and peace. I teach others how to free themselves from burden, struggle, confusion, stress and pain so they can release their past, trust their present and live their future with ease and grace.

This book will help you get headed in the right direction. You will learn the importance of choice, trust, perception, fearlessness, truth and gratitude, and I will show you how to harness the power you already possess within to live a life you have always wanted to live.

As you grow in this knowledge and your heart grows fonder and fonder of the person that you have become, you will be amazed at how much more love will be in your life. If this book teaches you anything, it is to know that you have the power from within to change your entire world. Live your life in gratitude, love, fearlessness, and most importantly, trust. Embrace it and live your life to the fullest.

In this book, I will provide tools and exercises to process destructive thoughts and harness your body's natural energy. You will learn new habits, thought patterns and belief systems that will nurture the life you want to live. When you release old negative patterns and nurture this new positive, empowering mindset, you will become open to many exciting opportunities for your future.

I will also help you identify the stressors in your everyday life that are difficult to recognize and perhaps even more challenging to accept. I can guide you toward wholeness and help you return to the feeling of oneness, the feeling that you are an awesome, perfect expression of you. Because interpersonal relationships mirror your vision of yourself, as you value yourself more and more, your bonds will either shift with you or shift out. It's all part of the process of becoming a peaceful, fulfilled you.

I am excited you made the choice to take this journey with me. You will find a power inside of you that you never knew existed. I guarantee you that it does, and I cannot wait to show you how to embrace and nurture it.

Let's get started!
Terrie Christine
Winter 2018

CHAPTER 1
The Gem of Clarity

"Becoming 'awake' involves seeing our confusion more clearly."
—Chogyum Trungpa

Anyone who has ever felt "rock bottom"—or has even been close to it—understands the gift that comes with that realization. To become whole, you have to admit you are broken.

The time has come for an awakening. It's time to release the regret, the negative self-talk and confusion from your mind and spirit. To truly achieve clarity in all areas of your life, you must shed the self-doubt and all the second-guessing you have been forcing yourself to endure. You deserve so much more than a life filled with misery and pain. Your heart is a treasure to be had—your worth, immeasurable. It's time to stop making excuses for people who do not value you and your soul. It is up to you—and you alone—to protect your personal peace. To gain true clarity, it is absolutely crucial that you guard your own tranquility—nurture and love it. When you have recognized your higher purpose, let nothing and no one dim your glow. You were born to broadcast a beautiful, radiant light.

There's just no way around it—we must walk through the tunnels of darkness during the most unforgiving periods of our lives to ever have the opportunity to bathe in the freeing light that awaits us at the end of each challenge. Trust that you will find the light; the darkness is not permanent. In fact, as you develop the practices made perfect through centuries of wisdom, practices such as meditation, you will learn and accept that everything we see and experience is always shifting, changing, disappearing and coming back into view. Take the tools I give you, work them, and learn to feel what it's like to be the calm center of the spinning storm.

You have the power within you to find the clarity you have been longing for. Clarity will come—it will align you and provide you with a clear, almost magnetic impulse that will guide you. Clarity will shake things up, shift your focus, and bless you with a momentum that will endure no resistance on its path. When you finally arrive at a place of clarity, the answers you have been searching for will be so apparent, you will never have to think twice as you move forward with grace and confidence. You will know without a doubt what's right for you.

Confusion is the First Step Toward Clarity.

Whether you are on the bathroom floor crying or dreading going home after work, it's time to realize that everything you need, want and deserve is all within your grasp—and it always has been. It is already within you.

You are wholly capable. If you embrace yourself, even in the midst of what you think are your shortcomings, you will find the strength to take stock of your life, your goals, dreams and challenges. Realize that you are not your past and that your future is unwritten. The only thing standing between you and what you want in life is your mind.

Let's be completely clear about something. Your past does NOT define you. You are more than what you judge as your flaws. One day, when the initial shock of rock bottom wears off, you will look back on times when you doubted everything—when your love life was hopeless, your job unfulfilling, your relationships one-sided—and be amazed at seeing the deep trench you were in.

It's those moments when you find yourself in the deepest trenches life can burrow. These experiences are necessary, for within the trenches is where an abundance of spiritual growth lies. It is in those trenches that you find out how strong you truly are and how much you can endure. That's the horrible beauty of hitting your low point; from there you rise. From there you learn you are a warrior, but were simply fighting on the wrong side.

I will teach you how to love yourself, to know what you want and need. Only when you know how to do this can you love others unconditionally. Everything in this life serves a purpose and presents some kind of valuable lesson—if we choose to accept it. Toxic relationships allow you to learn who and what you will accept into your heart and what you will not. Trust that when you cross paths with another human being, they are meant to be in your life. You do not have to force it. You are enough. You are worthy. If a relationship, either romantic or platonic, costs you your peace, it's too expensive. It will drain you. It's necessary to purge negative connections from your life. They are hindering your growth, blocking your ability to expand and preventing you from achieving the clarity you so desperately need in order to have a fulfilling life.

Detaching from unhealthy relationships is a part of living life, no matter how painful. The friend who was great at 10 may have grown up into someone you do not like. This can happen due to their own limiting beliefs that surface when they are triggered with life experiences. Move on with love and grace—but move on.

It's not uncommon to get trapped in a cycle of self-loathing if you feel you have made poor choices, hurt people, hurt yourself or found yourself on a path you never envisioned for your life. You must transcend those negative energies—let them leave so that the good has room to enter and take up residence.

The highest form of human intelligence is observing yourself without judgment and adjusting your thoughts, actions and reactions based on this new information. It's the first step in saying, "I am whole and at peace with myself. I love myself and others as well." Self-awareness is key to the new way you will be living.

Stop Watering Dead Flowers.

It happens often, that moment of panicked chaos, when you grab the phone and reach into the universe via friends and family to ask for advice to solve problems.

Brrrring brrrring!

"I went to my boss and you know what he said to me?"

Brrring brrring!

"My boyfriend left again! I can't get him to stop going out with his friends until all hours of the night!"

Advice pours in from all directions, some of it wise and some not-so-wise. You grab at it like you are drowning and react. Was your reaction the right thing to do? More importantly, was it the right thing for YOU to do? You are so quick to lean on others for answers and support, you do not even pause long enough to think about what you truly wanted to happen. You were dialing before you even understood what you wanted the desired outcome to look like. How can anyone other than yourself tell you how you should feel, act and respond? They may know you based on your relationship with them and certain feelings that you have expressed in the past, but they will NEVER know exactly the thoughts and feelings inside of you. From the moment you were born until now, not a single living soul has had the experiences you have had with the people you have interacted with in the moment of your life you had with them. However, we are asking others to help us with profound answers—and most will answer based on their own limiting beliefs and blocks they hold inside of themselves.

When we receive the answers we ask of others, how can those answers benefit us to our core when each one of us hold different limiting beliefs surrounded around different experiences? The answers from others will only be answers that would benefit their own values and beliefs and what they "think" you "should" do.

The fear of the unknown can be triggered so that we seek answers from others. Our desire to anchor into some form of awareness can create a false sense of truth when our answers are given to us by others. Your truth lies within. Trust what you feel and know without judgment.

Wouldn't it be convenient if all of life's biggest conundrums could be answered with a quick Google search?

Oftentimes when we are faced with a dilemma or a perceived emergency, we initiate panic mode. It is normal, and healthy even, to experience a little motivational, positive stress in pivotal moments of life. But your fight-or-flight mechanism often goes straight up to a 10 on the "perceived threat" register when the threat could actually be at level 2. (Our bodies are programmed to feel a sense of "disconnect" if we have not learned to connect to our own internal guidance system.) This space in time judges threat and makes split second decisions on whether you should fight or flee that threat. However, while your mind is working overtime, you miss beautiful opportunities to connect deeper into your own intuition to discover your unique power within.

An excellent exercise when confronted with this rising sense of panic is to just stop. As you feel the chaos rise, breathe your way through it. Quiet your mind of what you think the end result is going to turn out to be and analyze the situation, fully understanding what you want the outcome to feel like. Whatever you do, you must stop before you do it. Never act out of panic.

Part of this rise in "fight or flight" reactions has to do with our current world. When everything is beeping, pinging, buzzing and sounding, it is increasingly hard to discern importance and prioritize appropriately. Every angry word is not the truth; every decision is not an end all, be all; everything does not have to be done right this instant. You will always have the love you need and the clarity you desire.

When confronted with a situation that creates a strong—and perhaps panicked—feeling inside of you, here's a simple exercise that will bring you back into a more relaxed state where you can pursue clarity:

When you are in the middle of feeling like you lost your mind and your body is telling you to respond with a knee-jerk reaction, follow these simple steps to win back the power of you.

1. **Count to 7**
    1001
    1002
    1003
    1004
    1005
    1006
    1007

Within this first step, you can create enough space for your mind to SLOW DOWN.

2. **Take 3 deep breaths. Breathing in through your nose and out through your mouth**
This will ground your energy and create a feeling of stability.

3. **Focus on the Good**
By allowing your reaction to process through a grounded calm setting inside of yourself allows the rational mind to make the decision that is best for you.

If you choose what's right for you, how can you be wrong? Decisions that appear to you as a mistake or imperfection are not only okay, they are necessary for you to expand and grow into a higher purpose of living. Just as you would be kind and gracious to others, give yourself the same love, kindness and gratitude as you would give to your most beloved. When you doubt yourself or dwell on your past failures, you are not only hindering your own personal and spiritual development, but also doing a disservice to every single person you encounter—whether you realize it or not. This is judgment. When you harshly judge yourself, no doubt you are doing it to others.

Henceforward, there will be no room for toxic connections. Boundaries must be drawn. As you grow more loving towards yourself and your life, destructive interchanges become more and more unacceptable. You will find your newfound attitude attracts the positive and repels the negative; that's the beauty of having peace of mind.

If You Are Still Searching For That One Person Who Will Change Your Life, Take a Look in the Mirror.

There will come a day—although at times it seems that day is not to be found—where it will all make sense. You will reflect on all of your failed attempts at success and love, and the emotional aftermath. You will turn regret and disappointments around in your mind and understand why it all had to happen. Every single moment leading up to your awakening was necessary. You understand what you labeled as "mistakes" should be marked as "teachers." You will reflect on those who hurt you, wronged you, abandoned you and say, "Thank you." When you come to that point, you will experience the most euphoric breath of fresh air that has ever filled your mighty lungs.

Life will throw you curveballs and sometimes you dodge them, other times they hit you right between the eyes. It is in those very situations that you must trust your instincts, believe in your higher purpose and refocus your proverbial lens. In these moments, look within. What kind of reality have you created for yourself? What do you see? What do you feel? Does your behavior match that feeling? Are you living your truth? Are you speaking with love, forgiveness and graciousness? Do you look in the mirror and see the absolute perfect beautiful being you are, designed for a distinct purpose in an infinite universe?

Trust in the Divine Order of Your Life.

Things are not going to go your way all the time. That's why it is important to tune into your intuition and your unique feelings and thoughts. The hardest part of searching for clarity is in letting go of the urge to control. Your clarity lies in trusting the process, in feeding your soul with positive self-talk and in surrounding yourself with people who love, respect and nurture your mind and heart. Then, and only then, will you truly experience the flow, that feeling of "oneness" you want. By placing expectations on what you think the end result should be will only set yourself up for failure and create a constant sense of frustration.

As you encounter new challenges and are searching for answers, not finding them will teach you more than immediately gratifying answers ever could. Trust within the flow of circumstances. And, as you experience your journey towards clarity, embrace the uncertainty. There's great beauty in the becoming.

CHAPTER 2
The Beginning of My Journey

There he was, standing on the other side of the bar. He was exactly the kind of guy I dreamed about; tall, wavy black hair and long black eyelashes like those gorgeous Italian guys have. I was mesmerized watching him lean against the wall drinking from a highball glass. Several girls walked over to him hoping to grab his attention. One by one, he gave them little effort. It's as if he knew the drill. A smile. The hello exchange then the disconnected look as he scanned his eyes around the room, as if he were looking for someone. This time, our eyes met. He held the gaze and gave me a smile. As he slowly worked his way through the crowd walking towards me, I just knew I was a looking at the man that would change my life.

That night was the beginning of 14 turbulent years together. We began dating immediately. Our first year and a half together was pretty intense. Within the first five months of dating, I became pregnant with our first child. This was a surprise to everyone, including myself. I was 31 and had numerous reproductive health issues. In the past, I was informed by my doctor that I would have trouble conceiving children.

You may think that a woman who has had a long negative history around the process of having children would be excited to be pregnant. I, however, found myself lost, confused, worried and asking why this was now happening. I had so many things whirling around in my head—from having an abortion, giving the child up for adoption or simply having the baby and raising it myself. I knew I had to make a decision quickly.

I was raised with both a mother and a father, along with my older brother and younger sister. However, my father was a long haul truck driver so I rarely saw him, maybe once a month or sometimes more. As I was growing up, my world was wrapped around playing with my brother and sister and being cared for by my Mom. I felt that this experience left me with a sense of longing in the place where a father figure should have been. His absence created an imbalance in my life and, as I learned many years later, also in my heart.

When I got to the age where I would daydream about who I wanted to become and what I wanted my family to look like, I always saw a two parent household with a mother and a father who were both involved in raising the children together.

So, here I was, my worst nightmare materializing. I was finding myself pregnant in a fairly new relationship and having to make a life-altering decision. I needed to make a choice—whether to carry the baby full-term, raise the child as a single mother or terminate the pregnancy. All the while, I hoped the relationship I had with the man I felt I loved would continue. As the time to make a decision grew shorter, I found myself seeking answers from people I did not even know. I was so confused. I did not trust myself. As opportunities to speak with sheer strangers presented themselves, I found the strength to ask simple questions such as, "Have you ever been in a position of having to make a decision that could change your life forever?" and "What if I make the wrong choice?"

Can you imagine? I had so little clarity, I was wandering around asking strangers for their advice about having a baby. I can recall one instance when I went shopping with a friend. She went off to roam the store looking for something, and I was left standing alone browsing. Within minutes, a woman in her late 30s walked up to me and began a conversation. At first, our conversation appeared to be a simple banter back and forth. With each one of my answers, I would receive questions from her asking for my advice. She knew nothing about me or my own circumstance. This woman, who appeared out of the blue, began to tell me in detail about her sad and torturous relationship with her husband. She went on to describe how she was physically abused and could not leave him due to her lack of income. Then she asked me, "What should I do?"

In that instant, I felt a rush of relief. I was not alone. I was not the only person in the world who, when faced with making a life altering decision, felt confused and frightened as to direction. My overwhelming thoughts of confusion were disrupted by a total stranger seeking clarity in her own chaotic world. I was not the only one so lost in confusion as to seek the advice of strangers. I instantly knew that my decision was going to be made and that the end result no longer mattered. The only thing that mattered was the decision. The decision had to be right for me. Here I was, standing next to a stranger, finally getting enough clarity to decide.

My partner and I continued to stay together until our baby was three months old. At that point, our relationship was very strained and we both felt trapped. Yet, for the next 5 years, we carried an on-again, off-again relationship that resulted in me having another child with him and raising both of the children on my own.

I learned to adjust to the life of a single mother and sacrificed as I raised both the girls. My career was flourishing and the girls were happy, healthy and active. At this point, our oldest daughter was five years old while the youngest was three. Their father was making decisions to actively be a part of all three of our lives. He began calling weekly and talking to the girls on the phone for hours. I would hear the girls laugh so loudly when they were on the phone with him. I would sit outside their bedroom so I could listen to their happiness. He would ask to come over for dinner and, over time, he became a weekly dinner guest. That led to spending many weekends together too.

Our fondest times together were as a team of parents working together for the best interest of our children. After being on again, off again for 5 years, we made the decision to live together, and did so for the next 9 years. Three months before the end of our 14 years together, I found myself on the bathroom floor begging God to stop my beating heart. And this was the beginning of my own rebirth.

I spent the next four years trying to find the woman I lost. I had the opportunity to recall the type of woman I was as I went into the relationship. I was loving, outgoing, compassionate, independent and confident. At the end of 14 years, I found myself as an insecure, deeply saddened, lost and alone human being. What did I do to myself? How did this happen? I did everything I could to show him how much I loved him. I wanted the father of my children to be physically around as the girls were growing up. I was willing to do anything to show him how much the girls and I loved him. The choices I made drew me further and further away from the person I was. The choices I made were in the name of love. Or so I thought.

All of life is about choices.

From the moment you are born, you are making choices. Everything you do is a choice—and I mean everything. When you wake up, you choose to make your bed or not, you choose to take a shower in the morning or at night, you choose to eat a hot breakfast or cold, you choose to wear black or a color, you choose to leave your house to get to work at a certain time and you choose to have a positive attitude.

As you make choices through your life, you find yourself making choices for yourself and for the satisfaction of others. If you are not aware of it, you will find yourself making more choices for others than for yourself. Those decisions happen when you place yourself living outside of your own happiness. Choices made for others will be one more opportunity for you to say, "I'll get what I want or need next time." Those moments go from occasionally to sometimes to frequently to all the time. Those weeks turn into months. Months turn into years until you finally open your eyes and feel the resentment. For some people, the awakening never comes and they pass their lives, not having lived.

"Resentment is like taking poison and waiting for the other person to die." —Malachy McCourt

Resentment results from a wide variety of situations. There are two common sources of resentment a person feels in their life. One is: feeling used or taken advantage of by others. The other is: having achievements go unrecognized while others succeed without working as hard. Resentments often start and build up in the space where you are unfilled and frustrated—the promotion isn't happening despite your great contribution; your wife does not recognize how hard you work on the house; or conversations at the dinner table are always centered solely on your partner's work events. Insecurity, frustration, loneliness and neglect are a marshland in which these resentments breed and flow out into life, poisoning all your best intentions. Can you name the source of the resentment and trace it to its beginning?

Reflect on the times you put someone else's needs ahead of your own. How did it make you feel? Good? It is a selfless act of love. You should feel good. How about after the tenth or fifteenth time without ever receiving any reciprocation? As you continue to fill the needs of others without filling any of your own, it will begin to eat away at you.

If your never ending cycle of satisfying others first keeps you in the never ending cycle of frustration and hurt, this is your signal to push the stop button. There is a balance in fulfilling your own needs when you speak your truth to others as to what you want for yourself. Protect your happiness. Share your feelings.

My relationship with the father of my children was spent showing him how much I loved him. Year after year, I chose to ask him what he wanted before I satisfied my own feelings. I chose to accept that we rarely went out. I chose to accept that we rarely cuddled or hugged. I chose to accept that we did the same thing week after week after week. When I made these choices, I looked at it as a sacrifice of love. I felt deeply in my heart that the more I showed this man how much I loved him by giving up my own feelings, he could see how much I was willing to do for him.

What I did not know or understand was his perspective of my actions. He truly believed that I chose to give up my desires because I was doing it for me and only me. I chose to please him because that was making me happy. He did not think twice about my unmet desires because all his desires were being met. And if I do not say what I need, then I must be satisfied, right?

Maybe in his eyes, but not in mine. I was desperately needing someone to fill my needs. Yet I did not know how to arrange my thoughts, feelings and life in such a way that I could begin to be fulfilled and at peace. The fear of him not loving me far outweighed my own internal happiness. However, month after month, I resented him more and more for holding power over me.

How many times have you thought, "If she would just hold me, I would be happy" or "If he just cleaned up a little more around the house, I'd be happy" or "If he would help me more, I would be happy"? We have all done it, and the funny thing is that a lot of times we expect the people we want to fill our needs to just somehow know this stuff. The action to step into your own power is met with unconditional love for yourself and for your partner. As I learned, due to my own decision to refrain from speaking my truth, I caused my own internal pain. The clarity in filling your own needs is wrapped around the importance of knowing it's no one else's responsibility but your own. If you have a need, a want or a desire and you speak up to have it fulfilled, you are happy. You are not resentful that someone else is not doing it for you.

The responsibility for your own happiness lies within your ability to communicate what you want.

It is okay in a partnership to ask for things, because you both have decided to be a part of each other's lives. It is not okay to just assume that your partner should know what you need and want. Our perception with the experiences around us are so different. You could be cleaning thinking, "Man, I wish someone would help me," and your partner looks at you and thinks, "Man, she loves to clean. I don't want to get in the way." It sounds funny, but it's absolutely true. Your needs have to be met. If you need help, then you need to clearly state how you feel to your partner and how you would like to achieve a desired outcome.

But I cannot stress this enough: Never place all of the responsibility of your own happiness into someone else's hands. Speak. Ask. Explain in the most loving and open way possible. That is the beginning of true peace of mind—finding your voice in the middle of all the noise.

Choosing to please others first is your own undoing.

So many times, I hear how, "x,y,z happened and that is why I can't live the life that I want." It is heartbreaking to hear, but a common story that so many of us have had at some point(s) in our lives, including me. As common as this theme is, it does not have to be your truth.

It does not matter if you are at the beginning of a relationship or have been in it for years. By choosing to honor your own internal happiness, you will keep yourself smiling as well as everyone else around you. After all, people in your life are drawn to you; do not be afraid to show yourself and talk about what you need that makes you happy.

By owning every bit of your power, your energy and your soul—all substantial gifts you came into this life with—you are allowing yourself to move with more confidence, ease and grace in your life's journey. By "owning", you acknowledge you, as an individual, who possesses great abilities for change, adaptation and growth. The world does not decide how you live your life. You do. It's all about your mindset, your focus and trust in your choices going forward. When you take that power and make your decision, state it clearly and with love, you will begin to feel a power unlike anything you have ever experienced. You begin to be you.

Stay in the moment. Meditation is an ancient technique to reconnect you to the sound of your own soul moving. You can practice meditation anywhere, and should. Sit quietly and breathe in through your stomach, letting it rise. At the top of the breath, pause for a beat, release as your stomach deflates. Keep your attention on the breath. As you quiet all the voices in your head, the universe will guide you toward what's best for you. All you have to do is listen.

"Being present" is being aware of EVERYTHING around you—all sights and sounds close and far. By being mindful of your surroundings, you will receive answers to what you seek. The answer can come to you in various different signs: from laughter of children in the distance to an overheard cellphone conversation or even just a break in the clouds. These "signs" are all indicators of the answers you have been seeking, a kind of conversation between you and the Universe.

As you practice mindfulness, you will find more and more clarity. Clarity comes through asking yourself such questions as, "How do I feel about this?", "In what ways am I responsible for this situation?" or "What do I want the outcome to be?" Your feelings create the energy that guides you to that "little voice" we call intuition.

While rediscovering the you that got buried or cut off, love yourself. Stand in front of the mirror and tell yourself, "You're beautiful, valuable, lovable." It's not silly. It's true.

As with many things, magic does not always happen overnight. You must nourish it. You must believe that there is a better life for you and that you have the power to reach it. Little by little, day by day, the path becomes clearer. Walk forward. Breathe. Stay in the moment. Believe in yourself. Trust in the power of you.

Choose to take charge and follow your path.

As you experience life's expected and unexpected events, you make choices. The choices are what you think are best for you at that moment. As you are moving forward in your life , each breath finds you making decisions with the experiences around you. Some of those decisions may have placed you off the path that does not feel right to you or you begin to go through unpleasant situations. That's a clear sign that you have a past incident that you need to heal from or you shifted away from the energy that allows you to encounter more ease and prosperity.

How can people do a complete reset at 35 or 42 or 54? Seems impossible, right?

Not at all. They took guided action.

All around the world, millions are taking steps every day to improve their internal life. Those people then in turn improve the lives of all the people around them. And so it goes; for each person who becomes happier, so hopefully does the world.

You are taking guided action. Congratulations for that. You are now owning your power to make a choice. You are choosing to find your power and a happier, more satisfying way of life. When you choose, when you make decisions based on what you need, you will feel great excitement, fulfillment and purpose. You will be present and feel fully engaged and alive.

CHAPTER 3
Changing From Within

"Act the way you'd like to be and soon you'll be the way you'd like to act."

—Bob Dylan

Have you ever found yourself asking, "Why won't my situation change?" You are in a job that is unfulfilling and this is the third job in five years. Your children keep bickering despite the 3 times you sat them down to talk it out. Romantic partners feel unremarkable and nondescript.

You think that in order for your situation to change, maybe you need the people around you to change. If that's the case, it's up to you to find a way to change them. You spend months, even years, trying to come up with ways to show them they need to change. You ask, cajole, negotiate and plead, all to no avail. No one changes, nothing is different. You are exhausted and perhaps a little angry. But clinging to thoughts that if you just show a person how much you love them, they will change, is a quick leap to disappointment.

You enter relationships assuming they will be supportive and caring. It's a matter of common sense that if you thought anything other than that, you would not be going into the relationship. This pertains to all relationships; your relationship with your coworkers; your relationship with your romantic partner; your relationship with acquaintances; your relationships with neighbors; your relationships with merchants. Each relationship starts with getting to know one another. Over time, you determine who supports you and who does not. You assess whether the relationship has respect and mutual value.

You probably face your most varied and sometimes challenging relationships at work. Most of us work with at least several co-workers. For the most part, these will be good, supportive relationships; you are on the same team. Maybe one or two remain counterproductive to your efforts. When you bring your work conversations home, isn't it funny how your thoughts and words focus on the co-worker(s) with whom you have the most trouble? It's amazing the amount of energy we give to the negative interactions. You find yourself spending most of your energy either trying to get along, trying to get away, or even complaining about that person. Your perception has you viewing this individual as "tormenting you," "causing you pain," or "trying to undermine you." But most often, that is simply not the case.

For whatever reasons, you do not perceive this person as benevolent when you have little or no information about the person's thoughts, feelings and life. Perhaps they appear demanding and forceful. They keep to themselves the stressors of having three small children and a fourth on the way. Are they always grim-faced and exhausted? No one knows they care for their mother with Alzheimer's. In other words, people often have reasons. It's an opportunity to see others without judgment for their negative traits have nothing to do with you. These situations provide you with a chance to view others in a different light.

Your job is to change your perception; not the person.

What if I told you that it is not the person, but your perception, that needs to change? They are responding to the elements of their life. They need empathy, not confrontation, over a non-existent conflict.

Here's an example of what I mean:

Every couple of months, I would visit my favorite shop. Every time I went, I was helped by the same staff member. She was wonderful, but I could not help wonder why I was always being courted by the same individual when there were so many store associates. I knew the staff worked in a team-like atmosphere, and I knew they worked on commission, so I figured I would see a new face from time to time. On one rare occasion, I was assisted by another and was given a glimpse into just how the other staff members felt about my usual helpful store associate. It was clear that the others did not care for her aggressive manner. She hogged all of the potential client sales for herself.

A few days after that visit, I bumped into my friendly store associate outside of work. She felt at ease to tell me her personal history. Her story was based on a 25-year marriage in which her husband had not worked for the last 13 years, making her the only one in the family generating income to take care for his ailing parents. She confided that she worked two full-time jobs to make ends meet for her family. She hugged me and thanked me for listening and waved goodbye as she promised to see me again.

That encounter made everything clear. I understood how her co-workers could view her as being greedy and self-centered, but it was her own financial difficulties that created her need to do whatever she could to make money.

Perception would have been helpful to ease her coworkers' frustrations with her work habits. If they understood her situation, they might have felt differently about her personally and they may have felt a desire to help her verses hate her.

Changing your perception of your co-workers (and everyone else you find troublesome), accepting them for who they are, for the things we do know and do not know about them, will bring peace into your own life. Do not assume that their actions are directed at you; you can not see what you can not see.

Beyond problematic relationships, the office is full of many other challenges. Sometimes, the repetitive nature of a "job" can feel dull. Staying positive with your thoughts, words and actions keeps you focused on the good aspects of life.

Here are some great tips to keep you focused on the positive aspects of work:

Feel gratitude for:
- having a job;
- having other caring co-workers to provide support;
- having a place to fine-tune your skills and challenge your abilities; and
- having a position that allows you to feel good about yourself.

By focusing on the positive qualities of your job, you will help lighten or even change your perception of what you think others are doing TO you.

Find the lesson in every situation.

There are always two sides when you look at any situation:

1. Perception side. This way of thinking causes you to look at the situation with the mindset of, "This is happening TO me." What is the reason this is happening TO you? What did YOU do to deserve this? These are the questions you are asking yourself in this mindset. This thinking takes the power to control your feelings and responses away from you because you are acting in response to this happening to you.

2. Lesson side. When this perception is used, you look at the situation with the mindset of, "What is the reason this is happening FOR me?" What is the lesson you will learn from this situation? When you look at things from the lesson side of your perception, you take control of your feelings toward the situation and can look at it objectively. In taking this side, you harness your power to control your own reality. You use your power to change from within.

To get a better understanding on how this concept can benefit you, let me share a story about my client, Beth, as she learned to use the lesson side to take control of her life:

As a child, my client, Beth, was a "Daddy's Girl." The relationship between her and her father was a strong bond. Her Dad made her feel as if she was the number one woman in the house. He taught her how to build with her hands, working in the shed making furniture. He showed her the secret to running his business: sharing the design pieces he created for his clients. He talked about how he forged a relationship with his client to create a piece of furniture that would make their house a home. This bond was so deep between the two of them that he showed up at every single one of her soccer games, he went horseback riding with her and she shared her feelings and emotions unconditionally.

Her Mom created a different atmosphere. Beth recalled moments when her Mom verbally attacked her. She would voice her anger over Beth's shortcomings. If Beth gave her Mom a form to sign for school, her Mom would chastise her for giving it to her last minute. If Beth set the dinner table in a manner that her Mom did not approve of, she would make Beth reset the table while she shouted disparaging comments. The relationship with her Mom made Beth feel unworthy, useless and unsafe.

Over the years, Beth's Mom used Beth to ask her father for things her mother wanted her father to do. Beth became the go-between until the death of her Dad, when she was in her late 20's. Beth felt like she was a victim, tramped between two tormentors. The love between her and her Dad was unconditional and she knew he would do what she asked of him. She was committed to her Mom because she felt an obligation to be the daughter her Mom could love.

After both parents died, Beth found herself angry and powerless. Soon, she was caught in another "love triangle" with her brother and his wife .

As Beth observed, her sister-in-law appeared to be controlling and placing conditions that her brother needed to live by. As a result, her brother was in constant poor health. Beth came to me begging me to help her and her brother. Her entire focus on this situation was, "How can I get my brother to leave his wife to save his health? This is killing ME!"

Beth was convinced that her sister-in-law was causing her brother's deteriorating health and that he was not listening to her. Beth felt as if she knew the answers and could save him from his wife, if he would only listen.

As I pointed out to Beth, the love triangle between her, her Mom and her Dad was causing the main block in HER life. As a child, she grew to believe that her Dad would listen to her—she was the vehicle for her Mom's demands on her father—and by him listening to her, she saved him from feeling unwanted, useless and unsafe. In her child mind, she saved her Dad's life, and in turn, she placed this false belief into her subconscious.

Now, there she was, 20 years later, triggered by the same pattern and feelings her Mom and Dad created through the actions and words of her sister-in-law and brother.

Beth was able to see the link between the two experiences. At this point, I guided Beth back to the feeling that her Mom created within her. I asked her to forgive her Mom unconditionally for what Beth felt her Mom caused. By releasing the past, she was letting go of emotions that came with feeling used and remaining focused on everyone's needs but her own. When she understood what happened with her from her past, it helped her use her lesson side of thinking to address the brother and sister-in-law situation. Because she started using this new perception, she saw the relationship between her sister-in-law and her brother as something between the two of them. She would be the support mechanism for him when he chooses to step into making decisions on his own. Other than that, she would not get involved.

Beth's perception side: "Why do I always get put into these situations? Just like my father, it is my responsibility to save my brother."

Beth's lesson side: "I have learned that it was never my job to save my father. It was not for me to be placed in the center of my Mom and Dad's relationship. The same goes for my brother and sister-in-law. This is happening for me to be a support, not a solution."

Embrace the lesson and know that you have the power within you; you possess the ability to grow and expand so that your life feels less chaotic and more in balance.

Learn to let go and find the lesson.

You are born into a body with a soul that needs experiences to expand. You make decisions that sometimes kick you off the path that you came here to walk. If you ever get to a point in your life where you begin to question what is around you, "What is this life all about?" and "What more is there for me?", then you are beginning to wake up. Life is to be lived in ease, with love and gratitude. You will always have duality in life, with constant ups and downs. When you begin to embrace your ups and downs and view them as your moment to expand and grow, your life takes on a whole new vision. The ups last longer and the downs do not feel as low as they did before.

Everything that happens is FOR you to expand and grow. Those points where you feel low are moments to examine how you feel from events that caused unpleasantness. These feelings do not control or own you. These feelings no longer serve you.

Until you can make the decision to release what frustrates you deep within and search to find the lesson, you will continue to live in a cycle that has no end.

When making decisions, let decisions come from your intuition, an expression of inner knowing from deep within your being. Your thoughts alone will simply slow down the process of utilizing your intuition. Your head will want you to make a plan; think it out; rethink it out and think it out again. Letting go of control is scary, however it's often deeply rewarding, especially when you know you will be called upon often to make decisions. The true progression of mastering your intuition is trusting what you feel inside, loving yourself and connecting to the emotion about that decision. That is the way of a balanced life.

Whatever decision you make is never right or wrong. It is simply a decision that is being made. The important thing is to focus on how it makes you feel. If it feels heavy and dense, it's a sign that your body is telling you to reexamine the offer being presented to you. An example of this: You made a decision and immediately after you felt resentment or the feeling that you just gave something up.

If it feels light and right, it's a sign that your body is telling you that the offer being presented to you is more likely to benefit your highest good.

By allowing your body to guide you to the answers will improve your sense of trust. It's important that you eliminate the desire to let your ego answer. Your ego resides in the head and will take over the feelings from the body.

Relationships, disappointments and financial stress can go from feeling uncomfortable to unbearable. "Just dealing with it" does not work; suppress these feelings and they will haunt you with unbearable force. Resentment grows. Your attitude becomes more and more negative. People do not want to be around you. Your depression deepens.

Now more than ever, it's important to practice taking care of you.

This quote makes me laugh, every time:

"The best place to find a helping hand is at the end of your own arm."

It's so true. When you really need to do something for yourself, YOU are THE only one who knows what YOU need.

In the next chapter, we will discuss how you can break the cycle of discontent and get moving in the right direction.

CHAPTER 4
The MagStream Technique

> "If you will it, it is no dream."
> —Theodor Herzl

Working my way off rock bottom from the tiles of the bathroom floor took time, but it also set my journey on the course to save myself and others from these layers of pain and confusion that keep us from knowing who we are and what we want.

Just as you cannot build a new house atop the ruins of an old, you must peel back the debris that has built up on your soul before you can move forward. To access new, positive emotion—after all, this is why you hold this book in your hand—you must make room for these feelings. To live a new way of life—attracting like-minded supportive family, friends, and colleagues, not exhausting yourself on negative situations you cannot change—you must have energy.

As I regained my clarity and my life, I began to study tools such as meditation and visualization. In working with clients in search of their personal power and peace of mind, I saw the same emotional difficulties and breakthroughs. From this work came **The MagStream Technique**, a series of 5 steps that, if used consistently, will transform your life.

Here's how you begin:

1. Embrace the Negative

In order to appreciate the good stuff that happens in your life, you must experience what you feel is unpleasant. The small stuff that annoys you is not what we are talking about here. These feelings are the stuff of legends and epic films; these are feelings such as betrayal, abandonment and grief. If you are not careful, those feelings can overtake your life.

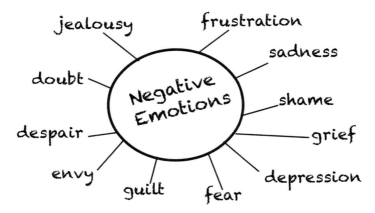

How do you embrace emotions that feel as if something kicked you in the stomach or sucked the life out of you? As you revisit the situations that generated the most painful emotions, your head automatically goes into your programmed pattern of "Why? Why? Why?" and your physical body goes into the fight-or-flight mode. This happens because your body is responding to your thoughts of being attacked or threatened. Your body now is on a mission to survive. That's why the mind is so good at blocking what is unpleasant; it's biology, a survival mechanism, and hard to override.

These emotions are your reality. Instead of running, embrace them. That's right, as you revisit a verbal attack from a boss, feel the humiliation, anger and unfairness. Really feel it. When you are mad, allow yourself to be mad. The same with hurt, disappointment or outrage.

Take your time. Allowing yourself to spend time with unpleasant feelings will provide the opening to the truth behind the emotion. As you do the work in step one, you learn that feelings come and go constantly, so feel and accept them. In fact, once the emotions pass, you will feel a rush of power. You stood in front of the things you thought took power over you. You allowed this power to fade into the night as the essence of you returned to feel empowered again. This is the first step in embracing your potential.

2. Express Gratitude

Gratitude is a remarkable tool for the human soul to reattach to the light. Gratitude is the feeling of being filled up, satisfied and at peace. I am reminded daily of the remarkable power of gratitude. Living in the lifestyle of gratitude keeps my mindset focused on all that is right before my eyes. It nourishes my heart with a feeling of abundance and that I am loved.

Many years ago, a friend of mine went through a difficult divorce. He was surrounded by friends and generated enough wealth in his career that if he chose not to work, that would be fine. He did not want the divorce and afterwards, his perception shifted so that he only saw what he did not have. After several years, his thought process turned to regret of losing the woman he loved and he complained his life was being manipulated by others.

Here is a man who admits that he has it all, but feels as though he has nothing. The fear and grief of the loss of his wife far outweighs his gratitude for anything else in his life. His thoughts are so fixed on what he does not have that everything around him became transparent and irrelevant. Yes, his pain is real, but the moment he chooses to let go, his perception will shift back. There will be room in his mind for the positive to flow in. He will see the immense riches all around him and change paths.

Gratitude can also function as a form of meditation. When you live in gratitude, your attention is placed in the present moment and your senses and emotions are heightened. You focus on what gives you positive feelings because that is where your thoughts are. The world becomes more beautiful. You hear more laughter. You feel more kindness towards others. That is the power of gratitude, and once it takes hold in your mind, an amazing circle of energy begins, drawing more positive to you as you give off the same.

By allowing yourself to live as if gratitude is a lifestyle, you will magnify your thoughts, words, deeds and actions, creating a positive outcome. Your comments to yourself and others will begin and end in gratitude. You will hear yourself saying such things as, "I'm glad for the job that I have," "I am grateful for this opportunity," and "I have tremendous gratitude for being in a position to help." Living in gratitude is a choice. How do you want to perceive your reality?

Here are some helpful tips to help you see all the things around you to be grateful for:

- As soon as you open your eyes in the morning, thank your pillow and bed for a good night's sleep.

- While in the shower, be aware and feel grateful for the warmth of the water on your skin and how magnificent it feels. We all know what a cold shower feels like.

- As you are getting dressed, feel grateful towards yourself for having the ability to purchase nice clothes that feel and look great.

- While driving to work, pat your car's dashboard for being reliable and allow the gratitude to flow through you, into your car and out to the universe.

- When you are at work, feel the gratitude towards yourself for being the amazing, skilled person you are.

- When you get home from work and see your children, feel the gratitude towards yourself and your partner for creating these awesome people.

There are thousands of moments similar to what is listed above. Start with choosing one and truly feel it.

"Gratitude unlocks the fullness of life. It turns what we have into enough, and more. It turns denial into acceptance, chaos to order, confusion to clarity. It can turn a meal into a feast, a house into a home, a stranger into a friend." —Melody Beattie

3. Ask For What You Want

Ask the Universe WWIT? (What Will It Take?) to achieve happiness, peace and abundance. Asking the Universe is the same as asking a friend, and, just like a friend, the Universe will answer. The Universe does not necessarily speak in words, but rather in signs, as we talked about above. An advertisement on the side of a bus suggests a beach vacation, the answer to your exhausted mind and body. Or, you see a butterfly fluttering past an abandoned business card on the sidewalk. You look at the card and a business or name jumps out at you and you make a phone call that changes the course of your life. You pass by a college and realize that completing your education is part of your WWIT. For everything you desire, ask yourself WWIT? This is an easy, yet profound way to set your intent for what you want in life.

Say aloud to yourself, "What will it take" and simply fill in the rest as to what you want to appear in your life.

Here are several examples of how this works:

What will it take to have everything I need before I know I need it now?

The answer for this one may come to you in many different forms, depending on the event. It works in marvelous ways when you least expect it. A client of mine uses this WWIT technique many times each week.

She purchased a used car and within weeks of driving it, she got a flat tire while on her way to work. She pulled off the road and got out to look at the tire. As she was standing next to the car, a police officer pulled over. He saw the tire and immediately asked if she had a jack. You see, she asked the universe to have everything she needed before she knew she needed it. She received help immediately without having to get frantic over her flat tire.

What will it take to release fear and pain and replace them with love and trust?

The answer to this will come to you so slowly that you may not recognize it. There are parts of your life that hold hidden fears. Some of these hidden fears may show up as contradictions. For example, you attract the same type of partner over and over or you yearn to be a writer while your half-written manuscript sits untouched.

All you know is that you are not making decisions that need to be made because you do not know what will happen, and not knowing is keeping you stuck.

One of my clients received the answer to her WWIT in a very interesting way.

This woman worked for a company where clients were assigned to her for representation. After working with one of her clients for several months, she felt she could not do anything right for her client. Her client challenged her every move and decision and she began to feel like she could never please her. Her client's demands were causing her so much stress that she began to think she was going to make mistakes. That's when she decided she'd had enough and began saying her own WWIT statements. She focused these statements on wanting the contract between her and her client to end and she also added that she wanted it to happen with ease and grace. As she made her WWIT statements, she trusted that she would receive her answer. Less than a week later, she was informed her client had a conflict of interest and was being reassigned to someone else. And as she asked, it happened with ease and grace.

Ask for what you want and be prepared to get it!
—Maya Angelou

What will it take to have a life rich in adventure?

What does adventure mean to you? Maybe it is more laughter in your life or you traveling more than you ever have in the past or going ziplining. You can even find adventure in simple errands you run. You may find that every time you are out and about something unexpected happens; you meet a new friend, stumble upon an impromptu concert at the park or walk into a new coffee shop and order the most savory cup of coffee made from beans grown halfway around the world.

Whatever your idea of adventure is, be mindful of what comes your way—you asked WWIT... you must pay attention to the answer as it comes to you. AGAIN, you will manifest the things you desire in your life, but it will be easy for you to miss their appearance if you are not being fully aware of what is happening around you.

What will it take to live the lifestyle of the rich and famous?

This WWIT is fun to play with. It has become one of my girlfriend's favorites to ask. It is not uncommon for the rich and famous to receive benefits for being nothing other than famous. They receive free items, free experiences, free travel upgrades...

It is not uncommon for travelers in first class to receive a free cocktail and a blanket to keep warm during their flight or to receive upgraded linens, toiletries, a mini bar and WiFi when booking a suite.

The rich and famous are constantly living a lifestyle of grandeur and, because it is their norm, their mindset keeps them in a space of expecting to receive these types of benefits. They expect to receive a first class experience wherever they go.

Similarly, you can create your own first class experience by using your WWIT statements to focus your energy and intent on receiving it. When you have the mindset of receiving, it appears. And that's how the magic happens.

Every time I have to travel, for example, I invoke this WWIT statement a few days before my trip. Again and again, I have received free cocktails onboard flights, free room upgrades and amenities at hotels, discounted transportation, free meals, free gift cards and even free services!

4. Meditate

Meditation is the #1 element that you must include in your life, daily.

It should be a habit like brushing your teeth every morning. We take great care of cleansing our bodies, our homes, our clothes and our cars, but we rarely take time to cleanse our minds.

With so much going on in life, our minds are always actively thinking and rarely do they get to truly rest. All the input from running the house, commuting, work, bills, the news, social media, planning the weekends, running errands, doing chores and the myriad of other responsibilities life demands of us, causes our minds to struggle to turn down the volume of the mental chatter going on inside our heads.

If you find yourself constantly living with thoughts of what's pending and what you need to do, meditation will keep you from feeling overwhelmed by the weight of responsibilities. It will also give you a sense of certainty and control and you will be much more calm during moments of high stress. In addition, when your mind is clear, you will be more open to the subtle answers you receive.

How many times have you come home after working 8 hours to be faced with cooking dinner for others; picking up around the house and getting the kids ready for bed; and all with your mind on bills higher than your income?

When you are constantly on the go, your mind does not have time to slow down to stop the chatter and rest.

If you are wanting to stop the noise, create a schedule where you take 15 or 20 minutes for yourself each day. This is critical self-care, just like brushing your teeth. No one can do it for you. You can either sit in silence or grab your ear buds and connect to your favorite meditation.

If you do not already have a favorite meditation to listen to, you can download a complementary recording of ThetaStream on my website www.terriechristine.com/thetastream. This guided meditation will take you to the deeper levels of the mind and leave you feeling refreshed and peaceful.

Next, take the first step of sitting in a quiet space to meditate and begin to ascend into your more relaxed state of being. Set the intention to keep your mind clear. An intention can be a goal such as perfect health or a question such as "What will it take to live with positive thoughts, words and actions?"

If thoughts of what you need to do tomorrow float in, just stop mid-thought and clear them away. You can simply tell yourself that these thoughts are not important at this time and you will get back to them later. The fact that you notice any distraction is a sign of awareness. Gently, but firmly send the intrusive thoughts on as you return your attention to your intention.

When you start meditating consistently, you will notice your mood change for the better. Meditation has many emotional benefits, including:

- **Gaining a new perspective**
Meditation frees your mind of continually reliving an experience and becoming stuck in what happened. When you finally stop playing reruns of a painful or stressful moment, when you observe the movie rather than starring in it, you allow your mind to shift. Once you have made that shift, your mind can expand and capture the story from another perspective. A range of possibilities opens up; by releasing the old, painful story you are then free to create a new story with a more positive outcome.

• **Increasing self-awareness**

Meditation creates a heightened sense of awareness and this allows you to examine with detachment how an experience made you feel. This leads to understanding on a deeper level why you responded to the experience the way you did.

• **Focusing on the present**

Meditation focuses your attention on the here and now. It removes expectations (of the future) and disappointments (of the past). It brings you back to the present into a place of mindfulness. The quote "That was then and this is now" illustrates this perfectly. In order to experience happiness, life must be lived each moment in the now.

• **Reducing lasting negative emotion**

Meditation allows you to look at experiences with a different perception and helps you open your heart towards compassion and understanding rather than closing your heart to stress, frustration or pain. You will still have your angry, sad or disappointing moments. The key is to reduce the lingering effects of an unpleasant experience by moving outside of the situation and becoming an observer instead of a victim of the circumstance.

5. Look In The Mirror

Too many people overvalue what they are not and undervalue what they are. —Malcolm S. Forbes

To love yourself is to honor your feelings, your desires and the things that make you happy. Self-love is the knowledge that you alone are enough. You will be loved for you, not what you can do for someone. How can you expect others to look at you with affection if you do not feel it for yourself? The most important gift you can give yourself is the gift of SELF-LOVE.

Whatever has happened in your life, whatever you may or may not have done, we are all perfect expressions of ourselves on a special, one-of-a-kind journey through life. You are remarkable, and it's important to acknowledge that as often as you can, or need to.

When you first start practicing this mirror technique, you may feel uncomfortable or even have an unnatural feeling. Do not worry; others have had this same experience. Pay attention to what happens. The more resistance you feel, the more this technique will amaze and transform you. If you do it daily, a strong feeling of being loved will begin to flow through you.

Here:

1. Stand in front of a mirror.

2. Look at your reflection pupil-to-pupil and simple say, "I love you. I love you very much. You are the one I love. I love you with all my heart. You are awesome and I love you. You know how to do so many things. I love you. You amaze me."

3. Give yourself 3–4 minutes in front of the mirror repeating these lines many times, in random order, several times throughout the day.

4. Keep practicing every day until it feels comfortable and the feeling of being centered and at peace permeates your life.

By feeling this love from within, you will discover that you no longer seek to fill a void. If you do not feel that void, you will not try to fill it with anything negative. The only void that existed in your life was the disconnect you had from your own inner love.

CHAPTER 5
The Power to Change

"Only I can change my life. No one can do it for me."

—Carol Burnett

Change can sometimes feel impossible. You live your life in a state of suspended disbelief; it keeps unspooling on the reel, but you are not feeling any of it. You are numb. Sometimes it feels as though you have tried just about everything to get what you want and need and no matter what you do, it just does not work.

What did you focus on when you attempted these changes? Are you the type of person who gets into a comfort zone and before you know it, it's five years later and you are still doing the same thing and still complaining about it?

If you find this scenario to be a theme throughout your life, then you need to start using creative visualization. It's scientifically proven that when you are thinking of something, others in the room or elsewhere can pick up on it. It's almost a frequency you give out in your energy, and if your thoughts are negative, then you most certainly will not attract a positive outcome.

So get creative about what you want to attract in your life and how you see yourself living it. Creative visualization is a form of generating a picture in one's own mind to generate thoughts that lead to feelings that lead to taking guided action.

Is lack a large factor in your life? Meaning you see many limits in and around your life keeping you from increasing your abundance. No college degree? Not a lot of work experience? No seniority?

Imagine yourself standing with a group of people. Everyone is talking and you are the center of attention. Everyone is listening to you. They are hearing you. They are doing what you ask of them.

You begin to FEEL what it is like when you are the solution. You are the one that everyone looks up to. This feeling generates a sense of trust within you beyond the limiting beliefs you tell yourself. You begin to live as though you are the solution and others around you respond in a positive way. You continue to trust and live as though everything you have and need is already part of your life.

Now, as you reflect back upon the limiting beliefs you had on the lack of no experience and no college degree, you will find yourself in the energy of having endless opportunities expose themselves to you.

So get creative about what you want to attract in your life.

You have the ability to totally transform every area in your life—and it all begins with your power of choice. When I asked the question of what you are focused on, there lies the hidden answer on why time stands still when having to make a choice.

Fear. You are afraid you will make the wrong choice; you will get the wrong outcome. That's all based on your feelings about yourself and your own worth and power. That's all based on the old stories you have told yourself.

As you develop a deeper sense of self and self-love, you will feel more confident. There is no right or wrong in making a choice. When you let go of the end result, you are allowing the universe to gift you whatever is meant to happen. If the thoughts in your head are placing limiting beliefs that you can not have the end result you desire unless something else happens, or that you want the end result to line up in a specific way, your thoughts will cause the end result to NOT manifest due to the limiting beliefs you place on that result. Simply make a choice and allow the end result to flow as it should.

Step into a choice with the joy of having the opportunity. Embrace the end result—and however it comes to you. This way, you are allowing the end result to exceed beyond your original thoughts when you tried to control the end result.

By believing in your own strength and trusting the power of your own choice, you learn what it's like to live fearlessly.

If you choose to live your life fearlessly, you will find that each choice and decision made will become an opportunity to expand and grow. Relinquishing your control over the end result will provide more opportunities to receive more than what you expected.

The power of choice to pursue your goals

I experienced this power firsthand when I decided that I wanted to take my intuitive life coaching practice to a higher level. For many years, I practiced as a part-time coach and decided that it was time to make it my full time journey. During the decision process, I instinctively analyzed each part of the decision and what would happen in the end.

Month after month, I became more unhappy with my current position. I was somewhere I did not want to be and wanting more and more to be where my heart made me happy. I wanted to be a part of helping people's lives. I hung onto the thought of, "How can I make this happen the way I want it to happen?" This process turned into another six months of causing myself more and more internal despair. I realized that my fear of failure was causing me to avoid making the shift into being an entrepreneur. When I identified my self-sabotage, I took control of my power of choice, let go of the fear of my end result, and chose to take small actions that would lead me to the final result.

If you have found yourself in this position where you can not pull the trigger to take that step toward your passion, here are the exact actions I used for my own personal power of choice:

- **Set dates to achieve mini goals that lead to the final goal.**
The first step is to break down an overall goal into mini steps that will accumulate into your achievement. Create a visual for yourself with deadlines so that you stay focused. By creating the steps, you are committing to yourself your own standards you can not escape.

- **Verbalize your intentions.** I began telling my closest friends and family the date of my last day. Making statements about my future made me more determined to keep my word. I am not a person who spews out random things. My words are intentional and when I say something, I intend to follow through with them.

- **Prepare your finances and lifestyle for the impending transition.** I spoke with my accountant about self-employment taxes and opened a separate bank account. Educating yourself as much as possible about the financials of your new life will help ease some of your worries and keep you from feeling like you are stepping off the edge of a cliff.

- **Practice your exit strategy.** I wrote a resignation letter to myself every week for months to create a feeling that when I write the final letter it would feel easy and say what I wanted it to say. I began counting the days within the last two weeks of my deadline date.

- **Let go of the expectations of the end result.** The day I resigned filled me with relief and excitement. The end result of my choice turned out to be better than I ever expected and both my former employer and I benefited. The fear of causing myself financial hardship outweighed my desire to succeed. When I finally let go of the end result, opportunities I never thought possible opened up.

Nothing ever got done without doing.

How often are you letting your fear sabotage your hopes and dreams? Realize that when you set a goal to accomplish your desires, it can turn into the outward energy from what you feel and believe on the inside. If you feel negatively, that's what you will emit, no matter what your words might say. That is why I ask you to embrace and feel your negative emotions in step 1 of The MagStream Technique. Once cleared of that, your mind has room for the positive thoughts that you will begin to welcome into your consciousness. That's what you will project, and in turn, you will attract the positive. Change comes.

The power of choice to make yourself happy.

Maybe you think you need to find a relationship because you believe there is a fulfillment that can only come from romantic love with another. Perhaps you believe that if you are in a relationship, you will never feel lonely or bored.

I have heard—and believed myself—the many reasons for "needing" a relationship. When you are saying these things, it is important to understand that these wants and desires must be filled by you first. You are responsible for your own happiness. If you expect another person to meet your physical, emotional and financial needs, you set yourself up for failure.

What you are doing is giving away your power to create the illusion of happiness. This is exhausting. Life is grand. There are no spaces that can not be filled by you. There is nothing that someone can do that you cannot do for yourself. Once you see the abundance in your life, all of the good, warm feelings you have created for yourself will fill the void you thought you had. Inside of your heart, you will feel happiness, laughter and abundance—by yourself and for yourself. You are all that you need. Anything else is the whipped cream with a cherry on top.

When you have created this for yourself and have decided that you want to share in these experiences with someone special, start from in your heart. All of that warmth and abundance within your heart is what generates the feeling of happiness for yourself. Only after you have filled your own love with love for yourself should you seek a meaningful relationship. When that time comes, stay focused on the love of more abundant experiences, more opportunities, more fun and more laughter. When these things are first filled by you and not "needed" from someone else, you will connect with your partner on a deeper, more independent, nurturing level. Love among equals.

Choose to focus on the positive, and let go of the urge to be negative.

What is the focus of your thoughts? What is it that you want in your life? In order for your life to transpire and transform, you have to decide first and then things move. Until then and by saying, "I have to have this in order to have that," how can you move forward waiting on something that you do not have? Does that make sense? The same applies with your thought patterns that are holding you back from love—thinking that you have to have something first before you can have love. Your focus should be on creating a thought and then FEELING what that would be like for you. Imagine being in a job that nourishes your soul, and then feel what that would feel like. Or the thought of having a partner that supports your ideas and beliefs, then feeling what that would feel like. The thought of having perfect health, and then feeling what that would feel like.

Set your intention and move towards it.

Focusing on positive and productive thoughts moves you into the energy of what it is that you do want. Find all the good stuff you love. If you are engaged and passionate, you will be a blast to be around. You will attract vibrant, action-loving people. Everything around you will feel great, including the bed you sleep on, the car you drive, the food you eat. Positive thoughts and ideas move the energy into designing the work you adore, having a home and loving family and friends who matter to you most.

The benefits when living in this happy space allow you to feel as if you are moving up and into sunshine. Your heart will feel like it's opening; searching for the light that nurtures your growth and helps you bloom even larger. This positive, happy energy will be infectious to everyone around you. Knowing that everything you want, desire, feel and crave is all right within you, is a powerful, joyful feeling. It's also infectious and soon, there will be other people attracted to you, and a field of blooming positive energy will spread far and wide.

Choose how you believe.

You find yourself flying out of the love canal and into the arms of a doctor where you breathe your first breath as a newborn child.

From here, you are living new encounters with each breath you take. With this child's mind, you have no experience to reflect back upon in order for you to make decisions. And with each occurrence, you decide what you like, do not like, want more of, less of, will never have and so on.

Your life experiences were shaped by your perception. And life experiences shaped your perception. Those episodes have now become part of your subconscious and are considered your limiting beliefs or blocks.

People who are stuck in these stifling belief systems often use limiting statements such as "I can't make more in my current job because I'm a salaried employee," or "I always attract the wrong partner," or "I'm all alone." These sweeping negative generalizations only hinder your ability to shatter these preconceived notions. Break this pattern and live free from the lies you tell yourself.

How? Go back and rework The MagStream Technique, for one. Secondly, challenge some of those circling negative thoughts right here, right now. If you find yourself circling around the same negative patterns, assess your belief system. It's always important to periodically reevaluate your current views to ensure you are growing and changing your thoughts. Change your thoughts, change your energy and from there, all wonderful things flow. If you want to reconnect with your beliefs, I encourage you to do three things:

1. **Identify your current beliefs.** What are some areas of your life where you have firm convictions? Examine the ones that you feel most passionately about. Do the people around you feel the same way?

2. **Assess what your belief does for you.** What type of energy do you receive from these beliefs? When you apply these beliefs in your life, are the outcomes positive or negative? Mixed?

3. **Establish fact-based beliefs.** Have you ever tried to find factual support for your beliefs? Do your beliefs HAVE factual support? Be honest with yourself. Rework your thinking so that it allows you to grow as a person.

Let us use one of the negative sayings above to explain my system to help you understand your beliefs. Let us use the comment, "I'm alone."

- So let's apply rule #1 to identify your belief: "I have identified my belief which is that I am perpetually alone. I have always lived this way."
- Using rule #2, I will assess how this belief affects me. "I am always alone, so I accept this and don't try to make connections with others. When I do, my negative mindset is off-putting to others around me. It does not make me feel good about myself."
- Let's finish with rule #3: "By keeping this belief, I close myself off to creating new and positive connections. If I let go of this thinking, I will be enabling myself to identify potential relationships. Just because I have felt that way does not mean it has to be that way. I need to make a better effort to create a change for myself."

You see how that works! Taking the time to identify a possible belief that causes more helplessness and negativity is life-changing. Give up a negative belief and watch the positive flow.

You are always going to have ups and downs, highs and lows. It's how you respond to the lows that allow you to truly understand and master your power. Unfortunately, our first reaction is often to run away from pain. Pain is essential for us to expand and grow. It will only help bring on change, if you let it. If things do not appear to go the way you want, there is a reason, and maybe that reason is not clear right now. Patience. Everything will be revealed when you trust. We are all stories in progress. There will be times that you struggle to get through or understand a situation of hardship, pain and suffering, but those are the times we do whatever it takes to find the lesson learned or create something positive out of it. It is a mindfulness practice.

Remember that you are amazing. Every single one of us will have a different result as to how we react, respond and receive. We process everything differently. Understand that this process takes practice and patience. What I hope you see is that this process works. When you set intentions, you can accomplish virtually anything. What you seek, you shall have. Work towards your goals in the way that you understand is best for you. By trusting the process, your life will be filled with joy, satisfaction, growth and learning.

Be like the mad scientist: Experiment, explore, research and ask. You can not push or control the answers. Allow them to flow.

Choose to take control over your perception of the physical things.

Sometimes with physical things, we just need to cut our losses and move forward. The most important thing to do is be mindful and take action, when appropriate. If you experience feelings and moments of trouble, use those results as an indicator that something needs to change on your path. If you do not choose to change the path that causes this struggle, you will continue to experience the same unpleasant feelings. Change and you are free.

When your life involves other individuals, you can not control their desires, wishes or choices. The only way you can influence the lives of others is through the example of your own life.

Creating change within your life can feel like an overwhelming process. Like many of you, you weigh your options based on your bank account. You see and feel that life is not going the way you want. But, with the bank account in play, you are faced with decisions between a much needed vacation and a much needed washing machine. Your thoughts tell you, "If I spend it, there goes the much needed vacation."

Your life is a process of thoughts, feelings and actions. When your thoughts are focused on limits, your life experience will be limited. You feel forced to live within the confines of a lifestyle based on the income. You create a balance to pay bills first and  the rest will go to necessities, like food and clothing. From there, you create a secondary list from the necessities and prioritize—what needs repairing or replacing and budging what's left over to buy more necessities.

And, as this story goes, your income is running the show.

This tangled thought process is based on your bank account—the "if I only had more money" approach to life. Your thoughts are so focused on your salary cap and the guidelines placed on you by the job that it becomes your Master.

Your thought patterns hinder your ability to see; your income does not run the show.

If you want more of something in your life then it's time to "manifest" it.

'What is a master manifestor?' Let me tell you how easy and simple this is and what it truly can do for your life.

A manifestor is someone who can create and manifest things in his or her life by truly trusting thoughts to create energy that brings what they want into their life.

Let me help you with some key points on being able to teach yourself or move into becoming a master manifestor.

Number 1: Trust.
Trust your thoughts that what you can have, you can create.

Number 2: Feel It.
Feel what the thought in your head would feel like inside of your body. Allow this feeling to permeate as if you already have that which is within the thought.

Number 3: Take Action.

Move into what it is that you are thinking and feeling by taking guided action.

Start with the thought that you may want, now let's say, to meet someone. Maybe someone special or someone who can create an opportunity for you. Think the thought of what you want to happen, then feel it within your body. Imagine you already have it and feel the great things its doing in your life. Run the whole scenario in your mind, thinking about it from beginning to end. See it in your mind's eye.

Now, take guided action on it. Tell other people, *"Hey I'm interested in doing something,"* or *"I'd like to go on that business trip,"* or *"Hey, I want to be a part of that team."* Whatever it is, mention it and create it. Feel into it, knowing you can do it. When you create the energy to magnetize your desired thoughts, you open up endless opportunities.

False belief patterns are passed down from generation to generation.

Let us take this deeper. The patterns that created your limiting beliefs are keeping you from reaching your final desires, which is the core of frustration. These patterns are generated from the false beliefs of your parents, grandparents, great grandparents and so forth.

Each generation continues to influence the next generation by their own false beliefs. Children hear their parents repeat negative statements; their reality is the child's. Money is a good example of how skewed beliefs seep down through the generations.

Start with great grandparents. These folks told their children things like: "Money doesn't grow on trees" and "Save your money for a rainy day." These might have been people who lived through the Great Depression. They also lived in a world of family farms, dry seasons and crop failures. They knew hardship and passed those fears to their children.

Then the grandparents used these same beliefs and told their children these same stories: "You need to go to college to earn good money" or "That's too expensive!" and the confusing, "Money is the root of all evil."

Then the children of those parents told their children the same stories. "The price of everything is going up while my income remains the same" or "We can't afford that!" and "I'd have to rob a bank to afford that."

Times have changed. Many of those beliefs came from life experiences almost 100 years ago; they no longer apply to our current economy. As the world changes, so should your belief systems.

What's your belief about money?

It's time to take a look at those deeper level blocks or false beliefs wrapped around money. If you want to change your relationship with money, taking guided action is important. It will also be essential to create a new story around your beliefs with money. Work towards attaching positive feelings of abundance rather than empty shopping bags.

These attitudes and beliefs feel like a part of your DNA, and in a funny way, they are. They also come from a skewed perception from THEIR experiences, not yours. If you have negative beliefs and feelings about many things—relationships, health, sex, career, and religion to name a few—your family tree probably held them as well. It is a powerful act to release yourself from generations of unhealthy thinking.

CHAPTER 6
Fearlessness Releases Your Forward Desires

"It is not the end of the physical body that should worry us. Rather, our concern must be to live while we're alive—to release our inner selves from the spiritual death that comes with living behind a facade designed to conform to external definitions of who and what we are."

—Elisabeth Kubler Ross

Imagine living life fearlessly. Imagine making decisions and not worrying one bit about what happens in the end. When you are living with unlimited boundaries, life is full of adventure. You are creating opportunities for yourself and with others. You are living your best life. You know because it feels so great. When you step into your endeavors fearlessly, you do not worry about the end result. Doubt no longer strangles your mind. You are allowing yourself to make decisions and move with intention to create opportunities that allow you to live bigger, bolder, and brighter.

When you allow yourself to use the energy that comes from setting positive intentions, you will find that everything turns out better than you expected. Fearful people can not do this. They toss at night thinking, "What if it doesn't turn out that way? What if I made a decision and it didn't turn out the way that I wanted it to be?"

So many of you walk around feeling you are being observed and judged; you are preoccupied with perceived "rules." There are no wrong choices—you are here to expand and grow. There is always something to be received from each choice, no matter the outcome. Being open to accepting the outcome makes the difference in the end result. It could be an experience of having to learn a lesson. It could be a false belief exposing itself to be healed. It could be a reminder to be grateful. Use each opportunity to shift into change and move into all that goodness that you want in your life.

When you trust in your abilities and the power you have to achieve your intentions, you will make the best decisions for you. Look at what you do see and ask questions to yourself to reveal what you do not see. What lesson do you need to learn? How can you change that into something even bigger and better for yourself? How can you grow and expand?

Take that moment to learn, reset and start fresh. I know sometimes these moments do not feel so great when they do not turn out the way you would like. However, after you get past the initial setback, look back and reflect on the experience. There is always an opportunity to turn any negative into a lesson. If you stay focused on your intentions, you will receive everything you want and more. You just may not receive it exactly when you want it or in the way you want it. That does not mean the universe has not answered in the perfect way. Trying to control the outcome will limit you to receive in an unexpected way.

Release your fears.

Fear of the unknown is one of the blocks I see in almost everyone. Making a decision and not knowing the outcome of that decision can be paralyzing to a lot of people. It is necessary to release the assumption you can control the end result. Whatever happens is going to happen no matter what. It is necessary to release any judgment or expectations of the end. Make a decision and feel that it is right for you. Know that when you are living in gratitude, use lesson perception, and work the five steps of The MagStream Technique, you can and will grow into this acceptance.

You will always have duality in your life; there will always be highs and lows. Be grateful for both. Be grateful for the highs and really enjoy the moment. Be grateful for the lows; there are no highs without them. Pain is also a wonderful teacher, as the saying goes. Extreme pain is the beginning of ecstatic change. So, when these lows come around, make the effort to evaluate them for the lesson. Ask yourself some questions:

- How did this incident make me feel?
- What could I have done differently?
- Were there negative thoughts or self-sabotaging behaviors in play? How can I change these?

Essentially, the essence of life is to expand and grow with our experiences. As you are learning those lessons, know that it's all going to be okay. You become the master of self when you learn how to respond to these lows. The master of self is the one who does not hang on to the disappointments for months. It is absolutely okay to be angry because this is life; this is human nature, and these are real human experiences and emotions. You can be angry and huff and puff and say a few choice words. Let it go. Give it space. Use your lesson side. Change your perception. Reset. Proceed.

Here are some examples of my work with clients and how they found the strength to overcome their fears:

Overcoming the fear of affection.

Suzanne was experiencing turbulent emotions in her life; she had trouble receiving help from others. She attracted assistance, but with that came troubled feelings. In her dating life, every time she needed extra help with a project around the house, a flat tire, or a retrieval of a large item, she found herself pushing away unwanted affection. These episodes became so predominant in her life she no longer allowed anyone to help her.

After working with Suzanne, we discovered that when she was in high school, she was forced into a moment of unwanted behavior from an older man. She chose at that moment to accept and allow what was happening in order for her to get past the situation.

Afterwards, she found herself projecting anger onto her body. She was angry at her appearance; over her curvy hips and full breasts. She felt that in her heart, she did not encourage that unwanted attention. However, a little voice in her head whispered in response, "any girl who looks like that is asking for it." Her emotions took over and she chose to blame something. That something was her body.

When we began to work together, she struggled with losing weight. No matter what she did, she could not lose it. Her relationships with men were all short lived. At the beginning of each relationship, her thoughts were always fixated on when he would make a sexual move and try to take advantage of her.

Our work together helped her to realize that she was not responsible for what happened to her in high school many years ago. In Suzanne's case, she needed to forgive herself for telling herself lies that her body was to blame.

She also needed to forgive her father, who was not responsible, however her thoughts convinced her that her Dad should have saved her from that horrible incident.

As Suzanne chose to forgive herself, this allowed her to release the guilt and shame of thinking she was to blame. This also allowed her to open her heart to love herself more. She remembered her old body with more affection and respect. She forgave her Dad for what he did not do to help her.

She had given these men a piece of her power. In forgiving them all, they no longer lived inside her, creating feelings of humiliation, stagnation and frustration. It's an interesting paradox, how we bind those we dislike to us with our strong negative emotions.

When you let go of the past, you are no longer a victim. You are free from the pain and suffering caused by past experiences that created painful feelings. You are free from harmful emotion and toxic personalities. You are free.

Overcoming the fear of speaking up.

The fear of "not being heard" can be picked up by a child in a very subtle way. In this case, Linda grew up in a household where her parents were attentive to her as a child. Her Mom did not work outside the home until the time she began school. Linda was an active, only child and demanded lots of attention. Each time Linda dropped something, her Mom picked it up. When it was feeding time, her Mom would bend over and pick up whatever food Linda knocked off the high chair. In Linda's memories of her Mom, she described her as being very attentive and loving.

Linda's Dad was the breadwinner, and she recalled that most of her interaction with him was loving and happened in the evening when he came home from work.

After working with Linda, we discovered that when she was a young child, her routine consisted of Mom spending all her time with Linda during the day, and when Dad came home, Linda switched her demands for attention to her Dad. As soon as he arrived home, Linda was there to greet him and play until dinner.

Every evening at the dinner table, her Mom and Dad began having a conversation. Linda was pushed aside to "wait her turn" after her father (male energy) had spoken. While her parents discussed their days with each other, she was left out of the conversation. This system or pattern created a subconscious feeling of "having to wait my turn".

As an adult, Linda's career was mainly male dominant. She attended management meetings where she lead the all male team. She described those meetings as a "struggle". She explained that a conversation would take place between her and several team members. Those members would discuss a topic back and forth as she "waited her turn" to respond. She became frustrated during most meetings because she felt her work mates did not care about her sitting there, struggling to jump into the conversation. It was disrespectful to her as team leader and a colleague. She would make a comment here and there, however, she was never able to feel as if she was a part of the conversation.

As Linda was able to reflect back upon her programmed pattern from her childhood, she could see the struggle that was created within her adult life. Once she released the limiting belief, she felt that her work mates were intentionally making her feel like "she needed to wait her turn", she was able to manage her meetings with confidence and poise.

Overcoming the fear of abandonment.

Fear of abandonment can be seen in many different ways, shapes and forms. Abandonment can be created in the mind of a baby who cries after waking up from a nap and the parent coming to the baby an hour later; the emotions of a wife when her husband of less than three years dies; the six year old who does not see her Mom again after her parents divorced.

A friend of mine told me a story about her much younger sister. She went on to tell me that her sister became angry after she left her in her apartment for 30 minutes while she ran an errand. My friend could not understand how her sister could be angry after being alone for only 30 minutes.

At this point, I asked my friend to describe her childhood and her interaction with her younger sister. She revealed she was from a family of 5 sisters. Both her Mom and Dad worked when they were growing up and her younger sister was brought up by all the sisters to help their parents while they worked. Many times, her younger sister would be left alone while all the siblings were doing homework or playing.

From this story, my friend was able to clearly identify how her sister could have been triggered with feelings of abandonment from her childhood upbringing.

Extensive studies have shown that a child, even before age 7, takes in negative experiences and feelings on a subconscious level; no one feels it being internalized. Years later—in their 20s, 30s, 40s and beyond—these early experiences can be triggered by the present, sending you down into a pit of negativity and hopelessness.

Sally's sister was experiencing a block. She had not fully felt the emotions of her siblings leaving her alone when she was young. I advised her that if she had friends or family members who are triggered with issues or feelings of abandonment, to talk it out with them. Tell them how much you love them and reassure each other you will not leave the other behind. Clearly talk it out with love and tell them how much you care about them. Help them to go back into their past memories to recall feelings of abandonment as a child, the exact moment if they can. What was the age in which you experienced this feeling? Helplessness? Lost? Alone? Go back in time and visualize who you felt this abandonment with. Allow yourself to forgive that person. Forgive anyone else who made you feel like you were abandoned and forgive yourself for the lies you told yourself about how no one loved you.

In order to release the pain of trauma in life, you must start with forgiveness.

Understand that when you finally allow yourself to be free of the energy of anger over what was done to you, you are no longer a victim. You are free. You are free of the pain and suffering.

Have you experienced pain so compelling that you choose to own it because you tell yourself that is what made you who you are today? These events are now embedded into your story of who you are and you walk around with this badge of honor to keep you from never having to experience this pain again. You think this condition you place on yourself is keeping you from having to live through the same pain from the past. The truth is, it is now keeping you from making each moment the most gratifying time in your life.

Little things can have a big lesson.

Sometimes, a minor annoyance can turn into a big enduring lesson. Below is a personal story about finding the take-away in my own negative situation.

I was driving to work one morning, many years ago, when my car broke down. That particular morning I had a very overheated, verbally aggressive confrontation with my daughter. It was not the best way to go about speaking to each other, but we let our emotions and differences fuel our anger and resentment. As I got halfway to my work destination, my car broke down.

This car was fairly new and had the many point inspections along with regular upkeep maintenance. However, this car with less than 20,000 miles somehow overheated. I chuckled to myself as I sat on the side of the road thinking about the current predicament I was in. Here I am, with an over-heated car after having an over-heated argument with my daughter. The lesson side of this story for me: stop and check your emotions before it is too late and you get "overheated."

I believe there are no coincidences in life. So think about what was going on before your negative experience happened.

- What were your thoughts before a negative situation occurred?
- Were your thoughts where you wanted them to be?
- How can you use this situation to get where you want to be?

Fear causes you to be cautious.

A client told me about her magnificent life! She's happy, has unlimited clients, and unlimited abundance. She creates products that she sells online, she travels when she wants, and has an amazing family.

"Perfectly happy," she explained.

I asked her some questions about her business: "How do you create? What do you do to create the many aspects of your life?"

She replied, "Oh, when I begin to create a product, I have a system. I have a process I go through in my head. I develop an online course from my teachings. I then review the end result and start to develop it. When I launch the product, I roll it out with caution."

Caution?!?! The red flags raised in my mind. I said to her, "Are you telling me that you are fearful of making the wrong decision?"

Bingo! Lights go off behind her eyes. She had no idea she chose to examine a decision so carefully that the energy of caution caused the fear of the unknown. What she feared was a negative or unexpected ending.

The word caution creates a sense of slow movement. When you are moving into a decision, it should be with ease and grace. Decisions are your free will at work. Having decisions to make is the hallmark of liberty, inside and out. Decisions are the stepping stones that move you forward.

Live life making decisions without fear. You have worked to get to this moment; it all flows from your talents and choices. It will continue to grow and refine as you trust more and go with what your gut tells you.

Release the fears about making decisions and move into them. Know that when you are creating; when you are working with people; when you are making decisions based on what you are feeling inside, it is really good. You are moving in the direction that's going to create what you want. Do not be cautious. Move forward and do it, even if you have to take baby steps.

Do not move your decisions outside of yourself. That is a short road to more frustration. If you get advice from family and friends and you feel it's advice you must take, then you are basing your decision on their own limiting beliefs and blocks.

Your thoughts, feelings and decisions create the reality around you. It is important for you to be aware of your feelings in your body, not just your thoughts. Those feelings in your body are an internal guidance system that tell you whether the decision you are about to make is truly aligned with your intentions. So be aware and know that any opportunity that is meant to be yours will be.

I REPEAT: Seek your own advice when making choices.

Listening to your own intuition is the cornerstone of life and lives are built on decisions. When someone else tells you what they think, it's all based off of their specific life experiences and what they grew up taking in, their programmed patterns and their limiting beliefs from their Mom, Dad, grandparents and whomever else was the main care-giver.

Your friends are telling you what they think based on their ideas of life. These ideas are "guessed" intents from their relationship with you, what you have told them, and what they have experienced with you. If your friend has ego difficulties, he or she might not even feel your pain. They will give you advice straight from their own life experiences.

Seeking this outside advice is not in your best interest. Your life is completely different. Your ideas are different. How you respond is different. What you think, feel and know is different. Asking others for advice will simply confuse you as you move into choice.

Most of us find ourselves trusting the answers from friends and family when we seek the answers we struggle to accept from within. Sometimes these answers maybe hard to accept or we have fear moving into a decision. Know that you already have the answer, it's about trusting what you already know.

I cannot say it enough: Release your fear and step into any decision you want to make. Do it because it makes you feel good. Do it because you feel it's for the best and higher good for YOU.

CHAPTER 7
Living in Your Truth

"Tune into your truth. Live it. Breath it. Beam it."

—Emma Kate

What is truth? Some say it comes from the heart. It's a knowing that evolves around the gut instinct that manifests from the inner most desires of what allows a person to grow. How can we live in truth when others are offended by what we feel is our truth? How can others determine what is right for us? Have they lived our life? Can they forecast what makes us happy? Living in your truth can be complicated unless you release the fear of what you think others feel about you. If you are living in your truth and it's coming from your heart, no matter what you say, it is always with love.

Are you telling others, "I don't want the truth, I can't bare to hear it!" when the reality is you do want to hear it? Do you want to live your life not knowing how your partner feels about what you said; how your co-workers feel about you or if you will have your job tomorrow?

Living in truth is speaking and acting in truth with EVERYTHING.

When you are afraid of hearing the truth, you may not like the answer. The fact is, we all want the truth and we raise our children to speak the truth. If you allow yourself to give and receive the truth, in the end, you will ALWAYS know the truth around all that you experience. You will feel it.

Truth is so powerful that people are afraid of the truth. People go through the most amazing hardships not to have the truth revealed; they dedicate their life to hiding. They hold back in a lot of relationships because of what they fear truth will do. A statement as simple as, "Sweetheart, what you said really bothered me," would open up a deeper line of intimacy. And if the person receiving this message does so by recognizing and receiving the truth and sincerity in their partner's words, they will respond in kind. They will say, "I didn't mean to do that. Let's talk about it. I'm not here to hurt you." Or, he or she will say something not so positive. Have the courage to say it and to hear it; it's important information.

Unfortunately, people choose not to speak the truth because they do not want to hurt anyone's feelings. But whose feelings really get hurt? The answer is the one who does not speak up. Live in truth. Tell people how you feel. Let what you think will happen go and speak up; it is being true and loving to yourself.

As you learn to speak what you feel, choose kind, non-confrontational language. Come from a place of love. You will be amazed how a few kind words can change the vibration in the air. You will be amazed at how you can change attitudes. You will continue to grow and become stronger and that's how achievers and leaders are shaped.

Allow yourself to feel emotions in order to move forward.

You have emotion and those emotions are very real to you. In order to understand the life lesson created by those emotions, you have to sit with yucky emotional feelings for awhile and say, "Okay, this is how that experience makes me feel and now I need to look at what caused this unpleasant feeling?"

Recall the last time you had this feeling. Go back to that moment and you say to yourself, "I am grateful for experiencing this and it no longer serves me." This will bring to the process a shift in emotions. Whatever made you feel different or uncomfortable no longer benefits you, and you can let it go. You do not own it. It was a limiting belief you created from long ago when you were a child.

Being able to embrace how you feel now is just as powerful as how you interpret your response. If you allow yourself to just feel first without action, you will be able to learn much about yourself and your life. With that, you will make better choices and flow in a more positive direction.

Think back to when I said certain negativity runs through generations. Be careful of the labels you have heard all your life: "She's my emotional child" or "He doesn't like people; he's always got his nose in a book!" As we grow and change, the labels someone hung on you as a child are no longer relevant. But many still hear those voices in their head, voices that keep them from moving forward.

Holding in emotion—not to mention the demands of your every day life—creates stress that directly affects your health. In addition, stress itself creates more negative emotion. What you think and how you feel literally permeates your body and affects you on a cellular level. This has been proven in scientific study after scientific study. Therefore, any part of the body can be damaged by prolonged negativity and stress. A famous study out of the University of California,

San Francisco studied the cells of young women who were caring for a developmentally challenged child in comparison to the cells of a group of middle-aged women. The cells of the young women had aged far beyond the middle-aged group.

As you let go of negative emotion—once you learn to de-escalate all the stress—renewed energy will flow back into your body; the exhaustion of unexpressed and/or battling feelings will not hold you down. You will stop bombarding your cells, your body will restore its vitality and the aging process will slow down.

Dr. Christiane Northrup, author of the landmark book, *The Wisdom of Menopause*, wrote, "Your beliefs and thoughts are wired into your biology. They become your cells, tissues, and organs. There's no supplement, no diet, no medicine, and no exercise regimen that can compare with the power of your thoughts and beliefs. That's the very first place you need to look when anything goes wrong with your body.

Walk *Your* Walk, Talk *Your* Talk.

By speaking openly about what's troubling you, each word that comes out will bring peace and relief. When you speak your truth, you are going to find major shifts in your life. You will find the words and the proper ways to speak your truth. It becomes easier each time you do it. In fact, in a short time, speaking anything BUT your truth feels impossible. Building conversations around the truth inside yourself with your family and friends feels like a whole new way of living. You used your power to release your fear of truth. Now you can focus more of your energy toward living a more truthful, purposeful, abundant life—a life you have always dreamed of living.

You want the truth, you want to hear how others feel about something, you enjoy fascinating conversations. Judgment turns social interactions into shallow chats about weather, gossip and status. When people sense openness and honesty, interactions gain depth. It's amazing what you learn about and from others as they tell you their stories. Those stories are pure gold; they should flow in and out of your life like sparkling thread.

If you have trouble speaking your truth, here are some handy ways to phrase thoughts. You speak your truth and leave the door open for others to speak theirs. When you live in your truth, you can have those really deep conversations about how you feel, how your Mom feels, how your friend feels; without judgments or arguments. Try this:

"Mom, I see it differently because these events happened to me. Though I disagree with you, I understand and support your position" or "John, we've disagreed about this since we were kids. I love you but I will probably never view politics as you do."

Disagreement and dissent does not mean that people do not love and respect each other. All it means is that in the wonderfully complex world, we are individuals, a unique blend of biology and experiences. Respect it. The person challenging or dissenting your beliefs is there for a reason. Listen. Speak. Grow.

When you start speaking your truth, be prepared for reactions; some pleasant, some not. Be prepared. Their words and expressions and behavior are not under your control. As long as you communicate, you process emotion. This is the way you build inner strength.

Speaking your truth in the workplace often causes problems for my clients—and for many others as well. I remember one client who told me a story about her colleague Harry.

"I was so mad at Harry because he didn't complete the project on time. He said to give him another hour; I needed his portion in order to finish my portion.

My usual protocol is to keep my frustration to myself. I don't want to ruffle any feathers, so I'm not going to show just how angry Harry's inconsiderate actions made me. I'll say "okay" like I always do, and ask him to get it to me when he's done."

This, I told her, is not how you should be living and speaking your truth.

You can express your disappointment without flying off the handle. Simply say, "Hey Harry, it was really, really important for you to meet that deadline. Next time, I will be sure to clarify what needs to be done and why it needs to be done so you understand the importance of the set deadline. This feels uncomfortable that I haven't met the deadline due to receiving your portion late."

There is nothing wrong with making your truth known. It's ok, it feels good—powerful even—to express what you feel. It's important to get the truth out because if you do not express how a situation makes you feel, then you will get the same end result, over and over. If you do not speak, Harry will continue to shrug off deadlines and your resentment will grow. Stress escalates. So does your workload. Not speaking your truth comes at a high price.

I say to my clients, "Your body will take care of what you can't." If you do not express yourself and release internal stress, your immune system will grow weaker and soon you will be dancing with serious disease. It's your choice; take it from the lesson side.

So it's all safe, right and good to expel your feelings by explaining how it made you feel. You are the master of your own universe. When you live your truth and express your feelings, it's important that you express all of them, whether it's anger, frustration, fear, pain, hurt, happiness or gratitude. There are no "proper" and "improper" feelings. Express the negative and positive—express it all!—and you will soon master balance.

CHAPTER 8

Mindfulness:
Transform Weakness into Strength

"Refuge to the man is the mind,
refuge to the mind is mindfulness."

—Buddha

Turning your weakness into strength is the act of shifting your perception. Did you know that being able to see what you may consider a flaw or a weakness allows you to lift yourself up in order to change into who you really are? If you are not creating the element of mindfulness in order to make those changes within, how can you even see it in order to make a change?

These weaknesses, or the labels of what you are calling weaknesses, may be moments that you can learn from. Why choose to run away from pain? Have a plan to catapult yourself into the energy and strength of who you are.

This strength is:
- Happiness
- Love
- Clarity
- Boldness

This strength is what makes your heart sing. It's what makes you happy to be in a job that is satisfying. It's what connects you to feeling happy when you are a part of someone else's life. It opens the doors to a clear path in relationships. It supports a healthy lifestyle.

When you focus your attention upon the things you do not want, do not know or even do not know how to do, this keeps you in the mind-set of being "incomplete". How are you going to get past that obstacle in the road?

A thought is the beginning of the creation of feeling. The first thought into your intent sets the direction to the desired result. You can maneuver your thoughts into creating this outcome by allowing your attention to be drawn into the actions around you.

Mindfulness is the act of focusing on all that is around you. You do not have to physically or mentally do something you do not know how to do. Take a look around to see the many different ways and angles that are being presented to you by being mindful.

You can actually manifest someone who can help or manifest the creation of a solution to get pass the challenges holding you. Or maybe just let it go and walk through those challenges another way.

There are things in your life that you want and you are looking in an endless circle. Perhaps it is a new job or a new partner—or maybe just some new excitement and adventure in your life.

If you are constantly looking for it, and your voice and your words and your actions are telling you something else, that in itself can keep you from moving into the energy of what it is that you are trying to create.

Here's an example: you could be saying to yourself, "I really want a partner to share my life with. I would love to have somebody in my life who makes me happy. We are laughing and going on adventures." These thoughts are active in your mind.

Meanwhile, you tell your friends and family several weeks or months later that you are frustrated that you are not meeting anyone and you will never find a partner. You tell them you have been looking and you just feel like it's never going to happen.

If you say to yourself what it is you desire and you move into the energy of that, the universe will move that energy, or your desire, towards you to allow that desire to manifest. As you are holding these thoughts of desire, it's like a magnet.

When your desires involve other people to enhance or complete your desire, you must release the limiting beliefs wrapped around how the final result will manifest. When your limiting beliefs become a part of the creation of the desire, then the desire will manifest at a much slower pace until you release or clear those limiting beliefs.

In between the time you thought within your mind your desire and the end result, the universe is gifting you many opportunities to unite you with someone or heal a part of yourself. You will begin to live in experiences showing you all of the blocks that are holding you back from that perfect mate.

When these opportunities are presented, if you choose to acknowledge them, they will create opportunities to let go of your false beliefs within your own internal triggers.

If you choose to look at someone else to blame and use what you see as external factors that keep you holding onto the thought that it's not you, you will continue to live on a merry-go-round.

The universe loves you so much that when you are asking for something and you are allowing this energy to move into your existence, these triggering moments that you experience will give you an opportunity to change within. This happens to help you see your own internal blocks or false beliefs and to allow yourself to learn from an experience so you can expand and grow from that.

There are many different ways you can look at these experiences around you. Allow yourself to focus on what you want, not what you do not want or what you do not have. Move forward knowing that you are taking guided action based on the interaction in meeting people.

Keep moving forward, because when you do, everything that you want will come to you. It's simply a matter of you keeping the pace and moving on your path.

Mindfulness will help you connect to yourself and with others.

You can be mindful in various different aspects of your life. Below are a few to get you started.

• Calm your thoughts

There are so many things that fly around in our minds -- to-do lists, meal planning, work and family activities—that our minds never rest. It can be hard to focus on your own needs when your thoughts are being carried away by every little thing. It's time to stop feeling exhausted and confused. So, find a quiet spot. Get comfortable. Close your eyes, and just listen to your breathing. Tense and release your muscles to get in tune with your body so that you can cut the noise out of your head. Just sit there and be with yourself.

Meditation is the mastery of focus. By slowing the breath, heart and head, you hear yourself living—you are focused on the now moment.

Focus on deep, inhaling breaths. Stay in the moment of air rising and passing through your body. You feel it. You hear it. Slowly, the mind stops its constant chatter and you are alone with just you. Thoughts may come into your mind to bring you outside of your internal silence. Simply say to yourself, "thank you" and let them float off. Return to your breath in this moment. While focusing on your breath, pieces of time fall away; you are being, not doing. Your nervous system quiets and your breathing is deep and regular. This is a peaceful state; it does not feel like anything.

• **Acknowledge and release negative energy**

Sometimes, there is something negative that is just weighing heavy in your mind. When you close your eyes, visualize bringing that negative situation to the front of your mind, give it a name and look at it. Acknowledge that this is a negative feeling that you are feeling and that it does not own you. Release this visual as though you are physically letting go of its hold on you. I sometimes envision my stressors as if they are attached to a balloon, and release it into the air, letting them float away from my mind. This type of visualization is very effective.

• **Focus your energy on positive thoughts**

You can get so caught up in what you think you can not do that you subconsciously talk yourself out of a lot of opportunities. Force yourself to speak encouraging words. Use words of affirmation. Congratulate yourself on the big and small accomplishments. It may feel weird at first, but I guarantee it will be exactly what you need to refocus your mind and thoughts. Repeat phrases such as "I'm proud of myself when…", "I like myself best when…", and "I like this feeling of….". Say the words enough and you will start to believe them. Take action enough and you become the person you want to be.

- **Bring your focus to the present—including sights and sounds**

In every present moment, allow your senses to multi-task. With your ears, listen to all sounds around you close and far. With your eyes, notice the existence of what is being presented before you. Focus on the present reality so your mind relinquishes its need to migrate back to the pattern of pondering over the past and the future. Your senses will heighten and you will see and hear new aspects of the environment around you. This places you firmly in each present moment to feel balanced and solid within yourself. In this state, you will see and hear many signs from the universe on questions you are seeking answers to.

- **Observe responses from others**

As you learn to see and hear with more alertness and accuracy, you will become sharper at accessing the body language of others. This is an important skill for navigating your path. Was that gesture too extreme for the situation? Are they overacting to hide or divert your conversation? Do they twist their body away from you when they sit down? Do their words touch upon the subject followed by darting eyes or a refusal to look you in the eye? Use this information in your decision-making. Mindfulness helps you access the signs all around you. Nothing is coincidence. Your intuition will tell you the truth from the information being presented around you.

- **Express gratitude**

Finally, remind yourself of everything that you are grateful for.

When you are mindful, you find clarity. When you find clarity, you understand what you want. When you know what you want, you can put positive energy around thoughts about it and bring it alive. This is a process from which abundance and choice flows.

Focus on yourself and how life is responding around you. When you use mindfulness, it is not a time to be wondering about what someone else needs or wants or thinks about you. It is YOUR time to be the observer.

Keep moving forward because when you do, everything you want will come with you and to you. It's simply a matter of you keeping the pace and moving on your path. If your attitude is "this or better," you will find negative, unkind people fall away; they will not like your upbeat attitude. You will attract happier, more successful friends and colleagues. The energy in the air around you completely changes.

CHAPTER 9
Grounded By the Power of Forgiveness

"The wisdom of forgiving : It does not mean giving people the license to hurt you over and over again. It is simply an act of releasing the pain others may have caused and remembering never to let them take away your PEACE again."

—Dodinsky

Are you trying to create happiness for everyone except for yourself? Are the calendar days changing however everything else remains the same? Do you believe that if you do not listen to what others tell you that love will never find a place in your heart?

This kind of thinking may be what keeps you from moving forward.

You have already recognized you need to find your power; you have the MagStream Technique and tools such as meditation, mindfulness and visualization. Forgiveness is another part of the equation for personal peace of mind and individual development; if you can not forgive, you can not move past the invisible barriers that trap you.

There's more at stake here than just your emotions and peace of mind. Not processing feelings of pain, betrayal, and abandonment can literally cut your life short. Negative emotion, as we discussed earlier, literally damages you on a cellular level and attacks your immune system, leaving you vulnerable for health concerns, depression and bad life experiences. Sometimes, the only way we come to understand our emotional distress is through our body ailments because that is somehow so much more acceptable. Make no mistake; your outsides and insides cannot be separated. You are a whole organism, body and soul.

So backward is our thinking about psychological issues, it was not until recently that medicine acknowledged there was no blood barrier into the brain. All the blood that processes through every little corner of your body moves through your brain. So why on Earth would anyone think the body does not affect the functioning of the brain? Just as physical distress can create psychological distress; the reverse is true. Emotional distress moves into the body and causes all types of symptoms. Left unchecked, you are looking at heart disease, cancer, high blood pressure, diabetes and more. All have a strong connection to emotion. Do not wait until you get sick to heal yourself. Address your emotions as they rise and let them go—the build up of negative toxicity and internal stress just does not happen. That's the BEST way for you to stay out of the doctor's office right now.

Even using a toxic judgmental word like "hate" in a conversation is like putting a screeching halt around feeling loved and fulfilled.

People run from that kind of negative aggressiveness. Any love you have created for yourself gets pushed aside and heavy dense energy surrounds you and your words.

You must forgive

In this order, you must work to truly forgive and release yourself from these restraints. Your forgiveness is about you, not the person you are forgiving. You forgive to be free. Their behavior is between them and who they might ultimately answer to.

1. Start with your forgiveness, for yourself. Forgive yourself for believing the lies you told yourself. The stories you know that are not true about your weight, your height, not being good enough or smart enough or even how could someone like you be loved by someone else.

2. Forgive the others. Forgiving others allows you to release yourself from the thoughts that you CAN NOT let go of, that cause hurt, pain or suffering. The embedded thoughts you continue to repeat keep your mind stuck in that moment in time. Forgiveness gives you permission to remove the shackles that bind you to that incident.

When you are ready to forgive, say out loud: "I forgive you all, I forgive me, I forgive everything that I feel you have done to me. I forgive you unconditionally. I see myself and others as their own programmed patterns and limiting beliefs. I believe it. I forgive you all."

A friend told me of a simple but effective forgiveness exercise she did whenever she went on vacation to the ocean. She would gather some shells or stones—whatever was around—and pile them next to her. She would sit by the water, pick up a stone and while she held it, she thought about a person who she felt had harmed her. She forgave that person and tossed the rock into the waves. I asked her how she felt when it was over and she always said the same thing: "Peaceful, free."

Release the pain, and when it's gone, what's left? If you can learn to move the bad out, the insides fill with only the good. That's what "unconditional love" is; bountiful endless joy.

When that pain is no longer there, what is left? Unconditional love.

Not forgiving can be holding you back from the pleasure of playing tennis, riding your bike, exercising, running and feeling healthy inside again. When you forgive someone, it has nothing to do with them getting away with what they are doing or have done in the past—it is simply unleashing you from the chains that are holding you back from what you want and that is your happiness.

After you have fully connected to your forgiveness, say to yourself, "I am love, I am unconditional love, I am happy and I am free." Saying "I am" is owning your power—say it often and mean it. "I am" states your sovereignty, your ability to choose, and your freedom from abusive relationships and emotion. "I am" is the clarity of owning your power and places you inside the existence of being just that—I AM.

You will glow with peace as you begin to resonate a different impression from your past hurt and pain. Those stories will no longer hold the intense emotions and you will radiate more love.

We all tell ourselves stories. We also grow being told stories of who we are and who we should be. Sometimes, these stories hide the truth. In your story, you may find being the victim is easy. If this is your story, you are a slave to it. Feeling the victim is a mindset that only deepens and destroys your own happiness.

Change the story. You have the power. As you discover it and learn, you will start living in your own power.

Let go, forgive, and live

By keeping the pain, no one will ever let go of the past.

Do you have a tattoo? Did you experience a little bit of pain or even a lot of pain to allow an artist to create something for you that you wear like a badge of honor? Did you know that your tattoo is similar to your limiting beliefs? That tattoo was created with the very same pretenses your limiting beliefs were created.

1. You experienced pain.
2. You placed this inside your body intentionally.
3. You wear it like a badge of honor.
4. It's a reminder of what you went through.

As that tattoo turned into a reminder, your limiting beliefs did the same. AND, those limiting beliefs are keeping you from moving forward into the desires you want. Reflect back and allow yourself to let go of what you think is your "badge of honor."

Forgive unconditionally. You will be amazed at how effortlessly you move forward in your life. Within this forgiveness, you will live in more happiness, abundance and freedom. Happiness is a shift away.

CHAPTER 10
Gratitude

"We can complain because rose bushes have thorns, or rejoice because thorns have roses."

—Alphonse Karr

Gratitude appears in joyous occasions. It appears when we least expect it. It appears when others forge a bond between our heart and theirs. Gratitude is elusive. It comes when we are pleased with ourselves or others; for many, it has strings attached. Someone has done what we want, someone has acknowledged our talent or worth, or we have received money or goods. But gratitude does not have to be caused; allow it to become a practice and eventually a state of being. Weave it into the simple pleasures of daily life as well as the landmarks. If you choose gratitude, you choose the good life.

Gratitude comes from the heart. Some are born understanding the concept, while others are taught in childhood. For many of us, the idea is novel and we do not know how to bring it into our lives. If that's the case, consciously integrate gratitude into every part of your life until you do not even think about it any more. It is a natural state of being.

Every day, take a few moments after your head hits the pillow to run through the day. Think of at least 10 things throughout your day that you are grateful for.

"I am grateful that I arrived to work safe and on time."

"I am full of gratitude to have good friends and a loving home to share with my family."

"I am grateful for the moments I spend with my children as the grow and develop."

End with a positive thought as you drift off to sleep.

The more you focus and express the positive aspects of your everyday life, the more your entire life will turn out the same.

Shift your mind into all that you do have versus all that you don't have. It is very simple.

When a friend gives you a gift of flowers or takes you to dinner, expressing gratitude flows with ease in response to the gift. Most of what you have in your life has been a gift. Take a look at the car you drive. It does not matter the make or model. You have a car, a car that provides transportation to and from where you want to go. This is a gift. You have a place to live, a home that provides shelter, rest and protection from the elements. This is a gift. You have clothes to wear that keep you warm or cool and food to eat. You have a shower with warm water, a refrigerator to store your food and electricity to run the house.

Take a minute to sit in your bedroom. Look around. Notice your bed, pillow, mattress, sheets, lamps, end tables, dresser and alarm clock. Each one of those items has a direct impact on your life. Each one aids in some form of good in your life. The bed, pillow, mattress and sheets create a soft, protected place for your brain to recharge each night. The end table holds your glasses, book and a bottle of water. The dresser organizes your clothing so you can get ready day in and day out.

Try this gratitude exercise anywhere you find yourself. You will have a whole new understanding of how gratitude can be part of everything that is around you and is creating a sense of fulfillment.

Why do we have to feel grateful?

The definition of gratitude is the quality of being thankful; a readiness to show appreciation for and to return kindness. What the definition does not tell you is that gratitude does not need to be a fleeting emotion. When adapted as a way of life, living in gratitude is a profound way to harness the most positive power inside yourself.

Gratitude is not a "thank you" for service. Gratitude is a lifestyle. Gratitude is a feeling of being full, a sense of peace, a belief you are surrounded by abundance. Gratitude is the sense your life is awesome just as it is.

How often have you felt "stuck" in your life? What were your thoughts and emotions? If you think about what you do not have, negative thoughts take over your energy and you diminish your own power. If you live a life fixated on end results filled with expectations, you are setting yourself up for failure. Make choices from the positive place of gratitude and let the end results flow.

Let us take a look at your thoughts and emotions while your life feels sluggish. I guarantee the number one question that pops up is, "Why can't I.........?" In order for you to create a life of fulfillment, one must experience accomplishment. In order to experience accomplishment, you must have an idea of what you want to achieve.

Formulate your intent through passion. Your newfound feeling of gratitude will open doors to endless opportunities as you focus on what you can and want to do in your life. As you live this lifestyle, feelings of being "stuck" can creep back in when you try to control the end result. Keep your heart open, make your choices and let the forces of the seen and unseen get to work.

Living in gratitude takes work and practice.

As you learn to live in gratitude, you will still encounter road blocks. Others will tell you what's good for you or a spouse does not support your choice for what make's your heart sing. Your expectations take hold and you feel defeated when the end result does not go exactly as you wanted.

Get back into gratitude as soon as you can after hitting walls. Say to yourself, "thank you for that lesson " or "thank you for helping me see how I was slipping back into my controlling ways." Think it over and over. Let it become your reality as you feel more grounded in gratitude.

Let me share some great ways to get you into the mindset of gratitude:

- **Be grateful for your reality.** Feel the juicy goodness for all you have. The best place to be in life is in the present. Enjoy this moment right here, right now for after this moment it becomes the past.

- **Place visual reminders around you.** Place sticky notes around the house as you work to shift your thoughts and rewire your brain. (Brain plasticity is the scientific study of the brain's ever-changing pathways and connections. Scientists now know that by changing thought patterns, the brain literally rewires itself.)

- **Remind and reflect.** If you find yourself sliding back into your old patterns and you struggle to remember to feel grateful, go back to your sticky notes and begin again. Reestablish what you are grateful for and commence with changing your thought patterns. Your brain is elastic and always in flux. There is no "never" with the brain; you can always create new pathways through just your thoughts.

- **Be grateful for missed opportunities.** If you come across a missed opportunity, close your eyes and say to yourself, "Thank you for allowing me to encounter this opportunity and I am grateful there are bigger and better ones out there." The more you live in gratitude at all times, the more the universe will give to you.

• **Start everyday with a big dose of gratitude.** Walk around the house in the morning and say "My life is grand. It's awesome. I feel great. I'm fulfilled and helping people. Things are just amazing in my life." When you focus on the negative aspects of "not enough money", "having to pay more money", or "Christmas is stressful," that's where your mind rests. Instead, focus on little things to be grateful for—soundly sleeping, taking a hot shower, cooking or feeding your children. Always focus your thoughts on positive. When you are living in gratitude, the universe seems to say, "Wow, look at her. She's living completely whole and satisfied in everything and anything. Let's give her more of that." That's what comes your way. More of that.

It's important to focus your grateful thoughts on EVERYTHING.

• "I'm grateful for my pillow."

• "I'm grateful to drink clean water."

• "I'm grateful that I can drive to work."

• "I am grateful for my health."

• "I'm grateful that there are people I can help." "Wow, look at the people that look up to me while I help them and they smile once I'm finished. I know when they go home, they feel better. I know I help their life."

For centuries, many of us have used prayer, chants, poetry, spoken word and the simple repetition of positive words to master our emotion and thoughts. The word "prayer" is defined as a solemn request for help or expression of thanks to God or creator or higher power. We now know that the sheer repetition of the words begin to change your thought patterns and in turn begin to change the neurological pathways in your brain, rewiring it. That's right, "change your thoughts, change your brain" as the scientist said. When you rewire your brain, your perception shifts and your words and actions change, even if you think they did not. When your thoughts are positive and open each time you repeat your chosen words, you grow stronger, more connected to the powerful joyful forces at work in the universe.

You are part of what you give to others. You do not need to hear them tell you they are grateful. You know that because you have learned to love and value yourself; you do not need to hear validation. You know everything you can do—your talents are breathtaking—and you are grateful for all of it.

When I work with clients, I trust 100% what I know, feel, see and believe. When my clients go home, I get excited because I know their life has shifted and transformed. I know.

I had a client struggling with her life. She was suppressing all her feelings and passions and she could not change. Isn't it strange how people stay unhappy and fight change? I pointed out that she felt one thing and was living another. I showed her how to hear her voice and trust her intuition. I wanted to let her know it was okay to feel it, let it go, and take a step forward. When she left after that first session, I knew her life was forever changed. I just knew.

I know that after reading this book and doing whatever it takes, you—and subsequently your life—will change. (Remember our WWIT?)

As you change, you will start to change the lives around you. That's the real joy in all of this; this is how you make the world better, spread positive energy and support others. Love as much around you as your heart can possibly hold.

Self love.

Loving yourself from within and gratitude are two essential elements to self love. Self love is valuing yourself and your one-of-a-kind talents in the world. No one else is you.

Gratitude should come with everything you think.

There are millions of things in your life to be grateful for—new shoes that look good, a delicious lunch, a cell phone that takes great photos and so on. Focusing on positive elements of your environment is the essence of life. You are acknowledging the things that you have in your present life to affirm.

Express gratitude for your body.

Gratitude can also help you release any resistance around appreciating your body. Limiting beliefs from the past can create fears towards seeing and feeling the goodness in your body.

Perhaps someone told you something negative about your body and you believed them. Mom called you "too fat" or Dad made jokes about your height.

Past experiences from high school may ring in your head; girls teasing you about how your body looked, the clothes you wore, your size. Based on the past teasing, you allowed yourself to believe the lies others told you, and now you believe "you can't wear it", "You are too fat" or "You will never look good in this".

Your body is the vessel that carries your soul and everything your soul needs to function. Expressing gratitude in every way in and around your body frees the negative limiting beliefs that were programmed into your subconscious about your body.

Spend more time lingering in the mirror, just look at your body, look at it unclothed and look at it clothed. When you look at it, look at your neck, your hair, your shoulders, your knees. We are all perfect as we are in this time and space. We then choose from this perfect space to eat healthier, adjust to a healthier life style, exercise or spend more time outdoors in nature.

Show gratitude by saying, "Thank you."

Whether it's a compliment about your shoes—shake your foot and say "thank you!"—to a well-deserved "good job," own the thank you and let it swell your sense of love for yourself and others. You are truly engaging, interacting and transforming.

It is all evidence you are wonderful.

When you live in gratitude, your mind fills up with your positive thoughts and the positive words and deeds of others. Self love, as well as love for everything, increases.

Conclusion

I hope that as you have been reading, you have started to put the ideas in this book to work. You already feel the magic happening. It can be a challenging path at times but it lights the way to a satisfying, joyful life. You will find clarity as you learn to release your limiting beliefs, let them pass through you and then make choices. Letting go of the end result of that choice leaves you open to what the Universe has in store for you; I promise it will be great! Release negativity. Everything—even if you don't perceive it as "going your way"—is a lesson that you needed. Feel gratitude and thank the Universe for all that you have, know and desire.

Above all, TRUST, as you move through this world in kindness, gratitude, fearlessness and love. This is the path to a better, brighter world. The Secret Power of You has always been there. Gift yourself the intent to use it as you master a love filled existence.

Acknowledgements

I am honored and grateful for everyone who supported any effort to get this book to print. You are priceless to me.

I, as my own master manifestor, have created endless opportunities for me to make a dream come true. I could not have gotten to the end result without the love and support from many of you. This book would not be possible without the contributions, love, teaching and guidance of many others, including you.

Ken, your infinite, unwavering encouragement lifts me like no other. You will always be that warm spot in my heart. Beth and Laura, you both shined your lights upon me so I could shine even brighter. I am the lucky one who got to experience "the cream of the crop." I could not have asked for a more perfect team as my editor and cover designer. Christie Marie, your love to make a difference in the world changed my life forever. Missy, your commitment to my ever expanding "gifts" and our great adventures together magnifies my love for you. I love you BIG little sister. Bex and Karen, as we have expanded and grown as one in the same time and space, I am forever grateful to you both for being there for me. Arialle and Meena, you both set the standard to the path of greatness. Janine and Mel, I'm overwhelmed with love for you both. We stepped into unknown territory only to succeed beyond our wildest dreams. Linda and Morgan, your continuous authentic passion allows me to just be me, thank you.

My clients and students, it is you whom I am in service. Your support and trust makes my life's journey all worthwhile. You, the reader, thank you for taking guided action. I wrote this book with you in mind.

About the Author

As an Intuitive Life Coach, Terrie Christine has mastered the ability to access her own intuition. This allows her to fully envision the struggle, hurt, fears and anxiety you are currently going through.

Terrie helps you change your life by helping you access your own intuition. She has the ability to help you release the pain from the past, realize more clarity in your future, obtain a feeling that life is easy or even improve the income you want.

Terrie Christine naturally works with the energy you hold to resolve your deepest issues. Her intuition is used to sense your blockages and help you eliminate the source of your pain. She then assists you by guiding you through the process of introducing new habits, thoughts, and beliefs that support the life you want to live. By healing these past issues and altering your consciousness, you can open yourself up to love and the abundance of opportunities that life has to offer. She can be contacted at www.terriechristine.com

Resources

Page 76

famous study out of the University of California, San Francisco studied the cells of young women who were caring for a developmentally challenged child in comparison to the cells of a group of middle-aged women. The cells of the young women had aged far beyond the middle-aged group

https://www.ucsf.edu/news/2011/02/9353/
aging-telomeres-linked-chronic-disease-and-health

Page 76

Dr. Christiane Northrup, author of the landmark The Wisdom of Menopause

https://www.drnorthrup.com/wisdom-of-menopause/

Page 93

Brain plasticity is the scientific study of the brain's ever-changing pathways and connections. Scientists now know that by changing thought patterns, the brain literally rewires itself

https://sharpbrains.com/blog/2008/02/26/
brain-plasticity-how-learning-changes-your-brain/

Books I have read that have enhanced my spiritual journey

Ask and It is Given—
Learning to Manifest Your Desires
Esther and Jerry Hicks

The Astonishing Power of Emotions—
Let Your Feelings Be your Guide
Esther and Jerry Hicks

A New Earth—
Awakening to Your Life's Purpose
Eckhart Tolle

Heal Your Body –
The Mental Causes for Physical Illness and the Metaphysical Way to
Overcome Them
Louise Hay

Creative Visualization—
Use the Power of Your Imagination to Create What
You Want in Your Life
Shakti Gawain

Letting Go of the Person You Used to Be—
Lessons on Change, Loss and Spiritual Transformation
Lama Surya Das